The Musical Theatre Composer as Dramatist

The Musical Theatre Composer as Dramatist

A Handbook for Collaboration

Rebecca Applin Warner

methuen | drama

LONDON • NEW YORK • OXFORD • NEW DELHI • SYDNEY

METHUEN DRAMA
Bloomsbury Publishing Plc
50 Bedford Square, London, WC1B 3DP, UK
1385 Broadway, New York, NY 10018, USA
29 Earlsfort Terrace, Dublin 2, Ireland

BLOOMSBURY, METHUEN DRAMA and the Methuen Drama logo
are trademarks of Bloomsbury Publishing Plc

First published in Great Britain 2023

Cover design and illustration by Rebecca Heselton
Stave © Tartos / Shutterstock. Musical notes © tuulijumala / Shutterstock

A catalogue record for this book is available from the British Library.

A catalog record for this book is available from the Library of Congress.

ISBN: HB: 978-1-3502-2941-9
         PB: 978-1-3502-2940-2
         ePDF: 978-1-3502-2942-6
         eBook: 978-1-3502-2943-3

Typeset by Integra Software Services Pvt. Ltd.

To find out more about our authors and books visit www.bloomsbury.com
and sign up for our newsletters.

Contents

Part Three Piecing it together in the creative process 183

Introduction

This is a book about building blocks: musical building blocks. More specifically, musical building blocks that are wholly bound up with dramaturgical ones; building blocks that can be used to build the construction that is a score for a musical. This book is written by a theatre composer whose main passion is musical theatre and who also frequently works with actor-musicians, composes music for plays and composes for media. Whatever the project, always, my aim is that the music tells the story. And I don't just mean the song lyrics tell the story; so often when we say a song tells the story and we analyse *how* the song is telling the story, we focus on the lyrics. I mean that the *music itself* tells the story, even if the lyrics were taken away. Music is a powerful language, but it is a non-specific one: it creates so much meaning and tells such a depth of story, evoking so much in the way of emotion, feeling, time, place and providing all the sensing ways that we know truth. But music struggles when it comes to specificity – it needs its verbal storytelling partner in order to communicate *exactly* what is happening in detail. Sometimes those details don't need to be known and each individual listener can create their own version of the music's inherent story. But sometimes it is important that those details *do* need to be known and such is often the way in musical theatre. Music and text are cohabiting storytelling partners in musicals, and while the two are often inextricably linked, this book will focus on the storyteller that is the music.

When music is so infused with drama, as it is in a musical, then there is a symbiosis between the music and the drama. Perhaps this is always so: perhaps music is always spun with so many infused meanings and interpretations, but certainly it is the case in musical theatre. Why not then extend this symbiosis to the language that we use to discuss such music? Musicological tools are incredibly important for the composer of any genre of music, and also for the analyst of music. However, context is everything and there is a very practical situation for the composer of musicals, that it is unlikely that they are discussing the score of a musical in *musicological* terms with their collaborators. Collaboration is vital to musical theatre. Even when an individual person writes both words and music, there will be someone they are collaborating with: a commissioning producer, a director, a dramaturg for example. Also, there are many composers of musicals who have not come from a classical musicological background – not all musical scores are created through notated music on staves. Ubiquitous sequencing software has also widely transformed a visual concept of music from the stave to lozenges on a timeline. Everyone involved in a musical needs to be able to talk about the music of the show in dramaturgical terms, whether they identify themselves as a 'musician' or not; a language that enables this to happen feels long overdue.

This book is intended for anybody with a dramaturgical interest in the music of musical theatre – for composers and those creating music directly yes, but also for those devising musical theatre and needing a way into the music; for those trying to find ways of marrying together character and music either as a creator, performer or director; and for those attempting to analyse musical scores from a dramaturgical perspective. In this book I hope to offer a language and some tools which can be accessed by all, whether you have a background in musicology or not. Musical theatre is an inherently collaborative art form, and it is important that we are all able to discuss the music in the drama and that these conversations are not just reserved for those who can read notation, or who are otherwise musically 'in the know'. There is no claim being made that this book gives *the* method on composing for musical theatre, or that this is the definitive way to approach a musical score. Instead, I offer some tools and ways of looking at musical theatre scores with the hope that you may find some of them useful and in the hope that it might strengthen collaboration in its many guises. I hope to offer opportunity for depth of compositional exploration for composers, and to offer 'ways in' and possible paths to discussing, analysing and interpreting music for those who do not consider themselves 'musicians'. I hope to offer building blocks for either creating musical theatre, or for analysing it.

By talking about musical 'building blocks', I mean that this book will help explore the various parameters with which we write music. We will be looking at structure – both on a large overarching scale and also on a micro level – melodic writing, harmony, rhythm and texture. As musical theatre creators, we make many choices all the time about our characters' expression of themselves and it is crucial that the decisions we make *are* in fact conscious choices which are dramaturgically informed. Each of these musical parameters (melody, harmony, rhythm, tonality, etc.) need to be decided upon from the motivation of dramaturgy, continually asking oneself the question what does the particular [rhythm] of this moment say about where this character/plot/storytelling is at right now? That is not to say that all of the parameters will be telling exactly the same story – in fact that is probably not what you want at all. They can be seen as multiple sides of the one personality, or multiple angles of the one dramatic problem being solved. Just as the music might be telling a slightly different story from the lyric, and thereby the combination of them reveals subtext, this can all happen between musical parameters – the expansiveness of the harmony or voicing might be telling you one part of a jigsaw puzzle while the insistent rhythm is revealing another subcurrent going on.

We will be looking at all of these parameters under two much broader umbrellas: **theme** and **shape**. These are my two mantras as a composer, working thematically to knit together threads of musical material over the course of a whole score, and using concepts of shape to help create contours of meaning within a show, within a song or within a moment. Think of it as working like a musical sculptor if you will – the themes are your clay or your marble which you are then moulding or chipping away at in order to create the dramaturgical meaning, messages and shapes that you hope to convey to an audience. **Theme** and **shape** are two shared languages; they are of concern to the entire creative team on a musical in a variety of ways and therefore we are going to explore them as the shared languages that they are. We will often be making reference to dramaturgical and narratological considerations, and Part Three will also encourage visual ways in as inspiration for the composer.

Before we start in earnest, a word about the term 'musical theatre'. The term is used throughout this book in the broadest possible way, and encourages an open mind as to what constitutes a musical. It certainly does not assume the West End and Broadway are what define musicals. It also does not suggest that they are not musicals. The terms surrounding the genre boundaries of any piece of work that brings together narrative and song have been hotly debated for decades. What is a musical? What is a play with songs? What is opera? What is music theatre? These are terms to be familiar with, but, I would suggest, to not get hung up on. The boundaries are ever-shifting, if they ever even really existed in the first place in terms of genre rather than cultural association. The ever-expanding use of technology in theatre and the new fusions of screen and live and hybrid theatre mean that the debate about terminology and genre could get even more multifaceted. The term 'musico-dramatic work', to me, brings about a helpful sense of neutrality and is more akin to where I sit on the matter: a bringing together of 'music' and 'drama'. If the musicals that appear in this book seem to suggest a particular definition of the musical, it is unintentional.

There are three parts to the book:

Part One works systematically through introducing concepts, tools and techniques: the first section is all grouped around ideas of **theme** and the second section on the subject of **shape**. This is intended for everybody, from creators and creatives to analysts. There are short analyses of examples from musicals given throughout Part One. All of the musicals selected are from the year 2000 onwards, and have been chosen to reflect a variety of styles and writers, and being mindful of the availability of resources so that the reader might have access to the material. At the end of Part One, Chapter 9 works through ways that the techniques might be put together to help conceive of a musical score, using the analogy of a series of maps.

Part Two focuses on putting these ideas into practice in a sustained way: Chapter 10 is intended for the analyst and undertakes a full analysis of the score for Dan Gillespie Sells and Tom Macrae's *Everybody's Talking About Jamie*.

Part Three takes on the guise of a workbook, and contains practical exercises, guiding the reader in putting the tools and techniques into practice while creating a musical. This part is specifically aimed at those who are composing or creating and devising music for musicals. Many of these exercises are intended for collaboration and might be used by a writing pair, a creative team, a devising group or might be used in the context of a research and development process. There are some exercises that are labelled specifically for the composer that deal more with musical nuts and bolts.

I hope that this book helps to excite the reader in the dramaturgical possibility of music and offers some inspiration and guidance in ways to find maximum joy in the fusion of character, storytelling and musical language.

The first shared language: Theme

Section One will focus on exploration of the language of **themes**. There are four chapters, each taking a different aspect of the umbrella subject of **theme**, and also arranged in the order in which you might come across these ideas in the process of considering a musical. We start with the 'way in' to a score, wondering what might be at the root of the music: a nucleus from which everything else grows. We then move on to consider the theme in narratological terms, and to explore the narrative of a musical and how that impacts the score. The third chapter takes a look at musical elements more specifically and introduces the idea of Laban efforts as a means of conceptualizing themes and characters in a show; musically, as well as dramatically. Finally, the fourth chapter takes these narratological considerations a step further into looking at large-scale themes of the show, and the resulting smaller-scale themes that arise from it, and the parallel with all of this in musical terms.

The musicals which will be drawn on for study in Section One are:

- *Billy Elliot the Musical*
  Music by Elton John
  Book and Lyrics by Lee Hall

- *Fun Home*
  Music by Jeanine Tesori
  Book and Lyrics by Lisa Kron

- *Hadestown*
  Music, Lyrics and Book by Anaïs Mitchell

- *London Road*
  Music by Adam Cork
  Book and Lyrics by Alecky Blythe

- *Six*
  by Toby Marlow and Lucy Moss

- *The Last Five Years*
  by Jason Robert Brown

- *The Last Ship*
  Music and Lyrics by Sting
  Book by Lorne Campbell

1

Finding the way in

The first question anyone will ask is, *what is your musical about?* As a creative of any variety, this is also our first question to ourselves. Embarking on a new show, the very least we need is some kind of concept about what it is about: an idea. Where do we now begin with a new score for our musical? How does that *idea* translate, from the composer's perspective, into anything up to ninety minutes or more of musical material? The 'blank page syndrome' is always scary and unnerving, and certainly in my world leads to much procrastinating, because waking up one morning and thinking 'I'm starting a new musical today' is just too big a bite to chew. Like all big tasks, we have to break it down into smaller units, and my first step is always about finding a way in.

Early decisions

Those early steps that a creative takes when starting out on a new score are crucial to the feel of the musical to come and not only can determine the nature of the whole musical score, but are also incredibly helpful to the process of the composer. Making some early decisions that set some parameters and boundaries for what the building blocks of the score are going to be helps to move beyond that rather scary 'blank page syndrome' and begin writing the music. Rather than embarking on starting to write songs in whatever style comes naturally, a composer needs some parameters in place to embark on a new score in order to help create the umbrella that will then help answer all the smaller-scale questions about the music that crop up throughout the entire process of writing the musical. What you are doing at this point is deciding on the very essence of the score: its fundamental roots from which everything else will grow.

The score needs to reflect what the show *feels* like – this is a very nebulous question but one that is so important. Inherent in this will be a question about style – what kind of sub-genre of musical style might this score be most related to? Of course, each composer or creative has their own kind of style in and of themselves as a creative, but the job of composing for theatre involves a degree of versatility to be able to adapt the composing process to the appropriate soundworld for the dramatic situation of the piece. It has been said that the score should sound like the set looks, and this is really a way of saying that the various languages of the theatre need to work together. A score for a musical cannot be written in a vacuum, but inspiration needs to be taken from the other creative decisions being made early on in the conceptualizing of the show – what will it look like in the broadest sense? What are the aesthetic choices? What is the premise of the show, and what decisions are made about the theatrical language of its storytelling and its relationship with the audience? However, in saying that the score should sound like the show looks, this does not mean that everything has to reinforce each other in giving the same cultural codes. This is a topic we will return to, but, for example, a musical set in 1776 can have a very contemporary score, as *Hamilton* has more than proven among many other examples. The musical score does not need to do the *same* job as other components, but does need to be driving towards the same overall vision of how the musical and all of its component parts work as a unified whole in their storytelling.

The answer's in the concept

How do you make these decisions? The answer to the seed of your score lies in the concept of the musical itself: the idea. There will always be something about the inherent dramatic choices that you are making about the musical that will lead you to the answers regarding the basic foundational building blocks of the score. It might be that you only need one element that hooks you in to knowing the direction of your score, or it might be that you build up a gradual picture of what the soundworld for the piece might be, based on a number of factors. We are going to look at three kinds of ways in to the score. There are, I'm sure, more categories than this, but these give a range of the kind of thing we are talking about. Here are some examples from my own experience as a composer of the kind of thing I mean by a 'way in':

Style at the core

Here are a couple of examples of show briefs where there is something about style that makes sense dramatically to take as a way in to the score.

Show Number 1

Show's concept: set against a backdrop of a fictionalized city where industry has dried up.
Essence of the score: the score draws on the soundworld of colliery bands as a starting point, exploring their timbre, harmonic language and textures.

This is an example of taking a pre-existing musical soundworld as inspiration because of its dramatic links.

Show Number 2

Show's concept: there are three lines of argument being explored in the drama of the show; it is set in Australia at the beginning of the twentieth century.
Essence of the score: each of the lines of argument has their own musical style.

In this example, it was appropriate dramatically, rather than to focus on the setting or time period of the show, to focus on the arguments that ran through the entire piece and were its dramatic organizing principle. Each argument therefore was assigned its own musical style and all of the songs related to each line of argument were in their characteristic style. At the point in the show at which these arguments find resolution and come together, the styles start to overlap and interweave with each other. At moments where the arguments conflict with each other, so too do the musical styles.

Both of these examples above relate to finding the essence of your score rooted in **style**. The 'style' of music is a broad term, acting as an umbrella term for a set of musical characteristics which come together in such a way that it indicates a particular genre or style of music to the listener, for example 'folk', 'R&B', 'legit musical theatre'. The setting, location and time period of your musical will be a helpful indicator for where the music might sit in terms of style, while remembering that the two do not have to match. There might be a particular dramatic reason, as in the case highlighted above with *Hamilton*, where you specifically want to sit stylistically opposed to the more naturalistic period and setting. The reason for deciding to do this will also come from the drama, just as the reason for making the style of the music align with the setting and period would; it just depends on what the whole creative team is trying to 'say' with the musical. The style of the music must make dramatic sense with the vision for the show and should be a container that then aids you in writing music that feels like it arises from your characters and their situation. Even if the score for your musical has an eclectic mix of styles (a show such as *Shrek the Musical* (by Jeanine Tesori and David Lindsay-Abaire) has an eclectic range of pastiche styles for example), then there should still be a high-level container of concept for the score that aligns it with the drama of the show such that the music all sounds like it belongs to the same musical, and does not become like a range of bits and pieces that does not sit together as a unified whole.

Style is very important to the musical *Six*. The show is a coming together of Henry VIII's six wives and so the factual period of their existence was the sixteenth century. The gig theatre inspiration in *Six* and the concept of the characters meeting outside of the framework of naturalistic time and space mean that there is no indication that a faithful approach to period would be suitable. Just as the costume design takes elements from period costume and incorporates them into contemporary costume, the score makes small tongue-in-cheek nods to the period, especially through the interweaving of 'Greensleeves' (allegedly written by Henry VIII) into a synth line in the instrumental parts of 'Ex-Wives'. The crucial nature of style to the score is not about period, but instead arises from the *concept* of the show. Each of the Queens takes on the mantle of a known pop-singer and therefore they each have their own style that aligns with the style of that singer. Writers Toby Moss and Lucy Hart have revealed in interview some of the musical influences on each of the Queens, such as Anne Bolyen's mixture of Lily Allen, Kate Nash and Avril Lavine's vibes (Official London Theatre 2019). The characters' musical identity is a huge part of their character identity, making six different styles the way in to the score. The umbrella style of contemporary chart-topping pop means that these different styles create a unified familiarity, much like listening to the charts or a pop playlist.

Techniques at the core

The next two example briefs move away from style as the key feature and look at very specific compositional tools as the way in to the score.

Show Number 3

Show's concept: a show all about the natural world and its cycle, with a view to righting the disharmony of the Earth.

Essence of the score: the score reflects the mathematical patterns found in nature, for example using the Fibonacci sequence as a compositional tool.

Show Number 4

Show's concept: a non-linear concept piece about the female spies in WWII. Morse code was crucial to their mission.

Essence of the score: the rhythm that arises from the Morse code of the show's name becomes the rhythmic building blocks of the whole piece.

These are both examples of finding inspiration through technique, using numbers and sequences that make sense from the fundamental elements of the show's concept in order to help find a compositional tool that can be applied across the score. This is an approach that relates more to the smaller-scale compositional process, as compared with finding a particular soundworld to inhabit for example. When using such techniques, it would be important to make sure there are other unifying parameters that help with the question of style so that it feels coherent dramatically, and not rely on maths alone. When an audience hears the score, they do not necessarily realize the specific techniques involved in this kind of compositional process – it's not because you want them to clock the technique – but it creates a particular sound that can't help but hang together in some way. It creates a great partnership dramaturgically between a detail that can be found inherent in the narrative world of the show, and the way that can bear itself out in the composing process. That can be very satisfying on multiple levels: for the composer; as a collaborative point of contact between all parties of the creative team; and ultimately in the overall sound of the score that has been created, born out of the same DNA as the drama.

London Road, by Alecky Blythe and Adam Cork, is an example of a musical score that is all predicated on a technique: verbatim. In order to portray the exact words of the people interviewed regarding the real-life story of the Ipswich murders, the score was composed with the exact rhythms and nuances of the recordings of the interviews. The manner of delivery of the score is presentational, creating a direct connection between performer and audience. The verbatim concept for the show inherently created the essence of the score; the rhythms, cadences and phrase details being created from transcription of the source material itself. Every hesitation and inflection is reproduced by the performers, with song structures arising through repetition of key phrases from the transcriptions; these become the building blocks.

The Last Ship is an example of a show whose musical core sits between both style and technique. Primarily, there is an amalgamation in the show of two styles: one rooted in folk and appropriate to the nature of the story of the shipyard workers, and the second a pop style very much recognisable as the soundworld of the composer of the show, Sting. Broadly speaking, the folk style is used for the songs that pertain to the story of the shipyard, and the pop world is drawn upon for the personal love story between Meg and Gideon. However, there is also a technical aspect which contributes much to the score, which is that a large proportion of the show is written in triple or compound time signatures. This is established from the beginning in 'Island of Souls' and runs through both strands of the storytelling – both in the shipyard ('The Last Ship' in its various reprises, 'Underground River') and the love story ('What Say You Meg?', 'The Night the Pugilist Learned How to Dance', 'It's Not the Same Moon').

Leitmotifs at the core

Here is another example brief:

Show Number 5

Show's concept: a traditional Christmas pantomime involving an adapted fairy tale and typical good versus evil tropes.

Essence of the score: each of the characters has their own theme based on their particular 'I want'. These musical themes are then developed, modified and carried through the rest of the show.

Thematic development will be discussed further throughout this book because it is a crucial part of the development of a score for a musical. In this chapter, I am raising it as a part of your potential early decision-making process – there are many scores where leitmotif construction feels like the right approach to creating the DNA and soundworld for your show. The term 'leitmotif' grew out of opera of the late Romantic period, and particularly the operas of Richard Wagner (1813–83). A leitmotif is a particular short musical motif (much shorter than a song – more like a phrase length) which relates directly to either a character, a dramatic concept (e.g. light or danger) or a more specific dramatic theme (e.g. the ship journeys onwards). It might be that your way in for a particular score is by creating short leitmotifs for your various key themes in the show and that your score grows through spinning them.

In *The Last Ship*, the opening number 'Island of Souls' provides a leitmotif for the community built around the shipyard of Wallsend, Tyne and Wear. The song provides some building blocks which return throughout the musical, some of which are melodic material which returns in 'The Last Ship (Part One)' and 'The Last Ship (Part Two)' and 'The Last Ship (Finale)'. In this respect it functions largely in the way that reprise does, through the return of material at key structural markers in the show as the narrative develops. 'Island of Souls', where the material originates, is an example of a storytelling song, where the community is established, and its return is used in other moments of storytelling. For the most part, this is not in the form of direct address, but rather where the shared community tell their story as the tale unfolds. The leitmotif here is a broad one, but one which encapsulates the vital role that community plays in the musical and the idea of storytelling that is central to the piece; a storytelling that initially is retrospective about Gideon and Meg, and Gideon's need to escape the life prescribed by his father. However, this storytelling becomes much wider than Gideon, albeit that his life and relationship with Meg remain of importance to the piece.

In *Hadestown*, there is dramatic reason for the use of leitmotif: Orpheus is writing a song throughout the show which will restore the seasons and bring abundance back to the land above ground. The song is based on a melody he heard from long ago, which was the song of love of the gods. Holding such a key dramatic part of the narrative, the leitmotif is used extensively in the show, and is adapted to different musical contexts in the show (see further discussion of this on p. 69). The wordless leitmotif is heard in the middle of 'Wedding Song', sung to 'la' as remains the case throughout the show. It is introduced very definitely within the narrative with Eurydice asking Orpheus to sing the melody for him that will restore the earth. In this iteration, it is the basics of the leitmotif that is heard and taken up in a choral iteration. *Hadestown* offers a very clear use of leitmotif which is intrinsic to the narrative. Leitmotifs certainly don't always have a diegetic reason for them as is the case in this show, but this is a musical which really explores that dramatic possibility.

On collaboration

These three approaches to finding the way in to the essence of your score may well overlap: it might be that you have a combination of conscious stylistic decision-making and also use a particular smaller-scale technique. I hope the point is clear though that these precious early steps in getting to know the character that is your score for your musical can be rooted firmly in the dramatic concept of the show. These decisions are something to discuss together with your team. Sometimes you might be commissioned to write a musical, and it might be a situation where there will be a clear hierarchy where there is someone's vision who originated the project. In this instance, these conversations are still continually needed but your role might be one of translator: how do the themes and concepts which are being discussed by everyone in the creative team translate themselves into a musical hook for you to be able to make a start on the score? If there is less of a clear hierarchy, or you are creating more of a devised project, then these conversations about the show's make-up truly happen side by side with your fellow creatives. The composer's input at this stage is needed as much as the words writer's: everyone is feeding in to the drama together. The composer's role as 'translator' is often a helpful analogy – right from the very beginning, you are seeing the (dramatic) world around you and thinking 'what does this *feel* like?' and growing out of that therefore 'what does this *sound* like?'

Other ways in

Interviews with the composers of a variety of musicals demonstrate that there are multiple roots to finding the essence of your score, each one of them taking something of the concept for the show and translating this into music. Each one of the examples from interviews below reveals an aspect of the composing process that is important to consider within the whole.

Annaïs Mitchell talks about how writing any song comes from a mysterious kind of inspiration that comes as a 'gift'. There is something that is the seed of an idea and then things grow from there, and so was the case with *Hadestown*. She speaks of the fact that Orpheus is a songwriter as being something that she wanted to follow further into the show. She states that one of the key themes in the show is that the song Orpheus writes asks a series of questions rather than statements, and those questions are all related to the song 'When the

Chips are Down'; literally the show asks the question 'what are you going to do when the chip are down?' (Talks at Google 2019) (see further discussion of this on p. 24 and p. 62). Finding a key theme and that providing a way in to the show is an important point, and one we will be exploring in detail over the next few chapters.

The inspiration that Annaïs Mitchell talks about resonates with an interview with Elton John in which he speaks of his emotional connection with the story of *Billy Elliot*, sharing some affinity with the main character in the lack of fatherly approval for his life choices. Having seen the original film, this inspired him in the songwriting for the musical. It is the strength of emotional connection to the piece that he cites as making the songs pour out of him and this is an interesting insight into the creative process. The element of inspiration is, of course, not to be diminished in any way in the context of a book which is about trying to create frameworks and tools for helping to write musicals. Often, creative inspiration will bypass all such tools, and it might be that the tools become helpful at the rewriting stage rather than the initial stages of creativity. It is rare that a show does not have to be rewritten and reshaped, often multiple times, and at this point tools and frameworks for troubleshooting can be especially helpful. Creating personal connection with your show is an important starting point though, and composing about something that you care about; whatever the angle might be, it is important to find your way in *emotionally*. In fact, in Part Two, we will look further at the notion of *feeling* as an important structuring tool for your musical. Elton John also states that his process is always lyrics first. This is an age-old question regarding whether music or lyrics come first, to the point that the question is something of a cliché. Everyone will have a different kind of answer to the question. However, I mention it here because for Elton John, that is a major part of his way in: he is always writing to someone else's words, and that in itself paves the way for inspiration. He also discusses the importance of writing for character, and how that defines the kind of feel a certain song will have (CBS 2008). This is a major topic, and something we will come back to in detail in Chapter 3.

Jeanine Tesori also speaks of her way into the score for *Fun Home* being about character. She speaks of the character of Helen, and the home of the

Bechdels being Helen's domain. Helen is a pianist, and so Tesori speaks of the sounds of scales and piano exercises that become a key part of Helen's soundworld. She contrasts this as an 'outer' soundworld of the house with the inner world, and Bruce's yearning and desperation for inner expression and the emotional soundworld of that. She then articulates the musical world of the children as being 1970s pop music, and the influences that they are exposed to, in particular being revealed in 'Come to the Fun Home' and 'Raincoat of Love'. Jeanine Tesori speaks of all these as strands of musical soundworld which then have to be organized and woven together structurally through the show (Playhousesquare 2016). This is an approach that will become familiar as we work through the idea of characters and themes and their musical equivalents.

Finally, Jason Robert Brown talks about the importance of the unexpected in an interview in which he discusses the score of *The Last Five Years*. Brown speaks of the inherent logic in music; that in a narrative there is a sense that the next unit happens and is 'meant' to happen, and that that same sense and idea plays out in musical logic as well. He describes his job as needing to question those expectations; why a certain progression has the expectation of moving to a certain place, and whether there are other places that it could go. He implies a richness of musical score that is created in this way, which is important to keep in mind, by challenging yourself and breaking out of conventional patterns (Bonnie Laufer 2014).

Summing up

As we have seen, the crucial first question – *what is your show about?* – informs everything that follows. Style, compositional techniques and leitmotifs are all examples of ways in to your score that all reel back to this question, and to the question of theme. And so, for the next three chapters we will be exploring different ways of thinking about themes and how this can result in musical creation. Seymour Chatman identifies the essence of story through two factions; events and existents (Chatman 1980, p. 44). In other words, we can look at the part that events in the story have to play, and also look at who is taking part in those events. As the interviews with composers have revealed above, ideas related to dramatic themes, and ideas related to characters are all crucial starting points in terms of inspiration for the score of a musical. In the next chapter we will therefore look at narrative and themes, and in Chapter 3 we will look in more detail at characters.

2

Theme, story and plot

As we have seen, the subject of getting to know the themes in your musical is fundamental to every member of the team. While we will be talking about musical themes, in a musico-dramatic work they can only ever arise out of dramatic themes, and so first we are going to explore the world of themes generally. Musical theatre is a temporal medium. Unlike reading source material in textual printed form, the temporal spacing of a piece of musical theatre, or its narrative time, is governed for the audience through its book and score. Through the various performance modes in the musical (words, score, movement and dance), relative weight may be given to particular moments, especially, for example, through the choice of song moments (often referred to as song spotting): one of the many ways in which a musical can highlight significant moments. We are going to look at how performance modes can govern the way that time unfolds the story being told in Section Two, Chapter 5. But first, because the score depends on it, we are going to look at the basics of the narrative itself. In *Story and Discourse* Seymour Chatman considers that '[t]here is in every story, regardless of its medium of representation, a portion which is *purely* narrative in structure, independent of that medium, that portion having its own structure' (Chatman 1980, p. 260). In other words, for the musical, whatever the means and performance modes by which the narrative is being told, and however conceptual the show might be, behind it lies some form of story. We are going to be looking at the way that composers need to know what the dramatic themes are in the show, in order to be able to also create musical themes. So first we need to work out what the major themes are to the story that the show is about.

Story and plot

It may sound obvious to say, but the dramatic themes *probably* arise from your story. There are two important follow-ups to this sentence though. First, is to understand what we mean by story, and it *is* story we are probably concerned with at this stage as opposed to the plot. In the field of narratology, 'story' means the underlying tale to the piece – as if it is somehow laying as the foundation to everything that we see happen. The word 'plot' then refers to the sequence of events that happen in linear time in order to tell that story. You will be able to think of examples whereby the underlying story is the same for a number of works whereas the plot differs between the adaptations. *The Last Five Years* demonstrates an example of the difference between story and plot given the way that it manifests time in the musical. The story is of Jamie and Cathy's meeting, marriage and the disintegration of their relationship until they separate, but the audience pieces this story together from a plot which does not give that sequence of events in a single linear fashion. *Fun Home* tells the story of Alison Bechdel and her relationship with her family, and in particular her dad, over a number of decades. The plot, however, tells the story by switching between different iterations of the main character in the form of a memory play, going backwards and forwards in time, and finding moments where these timeframes collide, such that the story is told in the way that memory operates: piecing fragments together. Thus plot, which would be the sequence of events story-boarded as they occur in the show, is different from the story timeline which is the real-life timeline of significant events that occurred in Alison's life in a linear fashion from a young age and through adulthood.

The other qualifier to the earlier sentence that the themes *probably* arise from your story is that it may feel like your show does not have a story; it might be that it has a concept instead. While *The Last Five Years* might arguably be considered a concept musical by some, there is still an underlying story. With the case of *Six*, on the other hand, this might be debatable. The musical does not really have a story in the sense of one that you could relate to your friend having seen the show, or to be more precise, perhaps it doesn't have a plot. There is not a sequential order of events or happenings in *Six* that mean you could relate 'this happened, then this happened …' but in fact there *is* a story behind it: the historical story of the life of Henry VIII and his sequence of wives. This demonstrates the way in which the story can be thought of as something that lies 'behind' what we see on stage or the more immediate, surface elements of what the show becomes.

It is this element of story in the early stages which gives the best clues as to the root themes of the musical. If your show is truly a concept musical or song cycle, as is the case with Ryan Scott Oliver's *35MM* that we will look at in Section Two, then your themes will probably arise from the sub-concepts that are inherent in your primary concept for the show.

But what is a theme? We use the term frequently, but perhaps a little more specificity would be helpful to our context. The language and terminology of the family of words which are related to 'themes' differ in detail from field to field. Even within those that relate to musical theatre, some of the terms differ in technical definition between the fields of literature and narratology and the field of musicology. Some of the terms have other meanings altogether in the world of science. Throughout this section we will be thinking of thematic material using metaphors relating to trees (trunks, branches, etc.). Let's start by thinking of themes with a kind of top-down diagram approach.

Universal theme

At the top of the diagram would be the 'universal theme'. In the one-liner version of what your show is about, this is it; this is what hits at the nub of your show. It's not the one-liner about the story *or* the plot; it's what lies beneath either of those things. It's usually called the universal theme in musical theatre circles, because it is usually something of fundamental importance that matters to a lot of people. Most musicals have something at their heart which speaks to the world at large – something which transcends human difference and speaks to a shared experience within the human condition. This universal theme is the largest, or highest-level, category of theme that we might identify in the musical and it's very important that we know what it is. *This* is what will provide the foundation for connection with an audience and will be a large part of the reason why the show would matter to people.

In *Six*, the universal theme is about female empowerment, and the women being able to tell their own story rather than their existence only being in relation to Henry as it has been for so much of history. The universal theme in *The Last Five Years* is about the devastation experienced in a breakdown of relationship. In *Billy Elliot* the universal theme is about identity, where Billy has to learn to grow into, and remain true to, his identity in the face of resistance and opposition. The universal theme in *Hadestown* is also centred around love and trust. The team have also discussed in interview the sense of universal theme around the question that is expressed in the song 'When the Chips Are Down', exploring the issue of what an individual does in that scenario on the understanding that this question speaks to universal human experience (Talks at Google 2019).

Theme

The term 'theme' on its own can mean the next level down in our top-down diagram, referring to the handful of broad ideas in the musical that run through it, that give it meanings that take it beyond the literal world of the stage and the show itself; ideas which relate to the world around us. It is likely that the themes might be related to the universal theme in some way; they may well be subcategories of ideas that relate to the universal theme or a number of different ideas that are being explored in the musical which all come together to make a whole. The term 'theme' is the word that runs most clearly and naturally across both dramatic considerations and musical ones: we talk of a dramatic theme and of a musical theme with ease in everyday conversation.

Some of the dramatic themes in *Hadestown* might be the idea of an eternal winter and **hardship** in terms of lack of food, and also in terms of working conditions on the wall in Hadestown; **destiny** in terms of Orpheus's purpose being to write the song that changes the fate of the world above ground; **mistrust** in marriage, shared between Hades and his need to have Persephone with him, and Eurydice believing that Orpheus will not be able to provide for them; **rekindling love** is seen in both the couples of Hades and Persephone on hearing Orpheus's song, and between Eurydice and Orpheus when he journeys to Hadestown to bring her back above ground. While the last two themes here relate to the universal theme of love and trust, the first two are not so closely linked to the universal theme, but rather bring additional strands of dramatic theme and give context and richness to the dramatic scenario that pursues the universal theme.

The themes in *Six*, however, do all mostly relate to the universal theme in some way. Ideas that are the opposite of the universal theme of female empowerment are seen through many of the Queens' stories, for example, themes of being abandoned, being compelled, falling out of favour with the King, which all point towards the final message where these themes of suppression are reversed to deliver a message of empowerment. In this instance, the majority of the themes in the show all move towards conveying the central, universal theme, but as we can see from the example of *Hadestown*, these links are not always direct ones. The variety of main themes weaves together like a tapestry to give different thematic dimensions to the overall issue of the show.

Motifs

The term 'theme' can be used to refer to a musical theme as much as a dramatic one. It may well be the case, as we shall explore in Chapter 4, that these are linked: that a musical theme might be related to a unit of thematic material running through the show. We discussed a version of this in the previous chapter in terms of leitmotifs, where a particular phrase of music is linked with a dramatic meaning.

On the next layer down in the top-down diagram we come to what we might call 'motifs'. In a musicological sense, a motif might be smaller than a theme – it might be a shorter phrase length or unit of musical material. Perhaps a theme might be made up of multiple motifs used at different times in the show, or in combination with each other. Or perhaps there is just one motif which is linked with a dramatic theme, in the way that leitmotifs operate. In *Hadestown*, the first phrase of the wordless line that the Fates sing to 'Ooo' in 'Any Way the

Wind Blows' might be considered a motif. It returns to signify the wind and the sense of impending lack and hardship.

Cells

Finally, of even smaller size is the 'cell'. A cell might be made up of no more than two notes, creating one distinctive interval which is then used throughout the work with intentional significance. For example, in *London Road*, the cell on the word 'yeah' in 'It Could Be Him' becomes a repeating cell in its own right. A cell might be harmonic or accompanimental as much as melodic. For example, the vamp that is heard at the beginning of 'Island of Souls' in *The Last Ship* is made up of two cells that repeat as an accompanimental pattern with shifting harmony: the first is a cell of a rising minor third, and the second a cell of a falling tone.

In this chapter so far we have been using words that imply that material carries *meaning* with it. So, at this point we are going to divert for a moment to briefly look at a theoretical concept that helps explain how we create, or interpret, meaning: semiotics. Semiotics and, indeed, *meaning* are large academic fields of study which could occupy us for a great deal of time, but it is helpful for us to have a basic understanding of its principles in order to give further depth to our consideration of thematic work.

A brief introduction to semiotics

Ferdinand de Saussure (1857–1913) instigated the beginnings of current ideas of semiotics through his conceptualization of a sign system surrounding linguistics. The basics of the idea are that we interpret meaning through 'signs'. In a Saussurean framework a sign has two parts: the signifier and the signified. While the signifier has a material existence, the signified is the conceptual part of the sign and so, for example, the utterance of the word 'flame' is the signifier while the idea brought to mind of the way an ignited candle looks is the signified, and for Saussure *this* is its 'meaning'. To attach any *value* to that meaning in Saussurean terms is a process of exchange within the sign system, whereby the example of the illuminated candle might then be exchanged for the meaning of a lighted candle signifying an intimate dinner, a power cut, or a religious service taking place. Roland Barthes (1915–80) built upon Saussure's method resulting in the idea of a 'semiological chain' (Barthes 2000, pp. 111–17) in which the signifier and the signified as one sign become the signifier for the next sign in the chain. As such the example of the lighted candle may, for instance, have taken on religious connotation, which then forwards in the chain to the representation of divine light of the world. I have used this particular example to demonstrate how the semiological chain can escalate in scale of meaning through to what Rick Knowles calls 'the global sign' (Knowles 2014, p. 26). Through such a system of signs 'the global sign' can be reached which demonstrates a central message: essentially the universal theme that we talked about above.

Whereas in linguistics the signifier might be the utterance of the word and the signified is its visual presence, as detailed above, when we transfer that idea over to musical theatre, it is not an exact science. Rather, the main idea to carry forward is the two-step idea that there is *something* (the signifier) which carries with it potential meaning (the signified). I say *potential* meaning because signifiers often have multiple potential meanings, and not everybody interprets things in the same way.

The anthropologist Claude Lévi-Strauss proposed that 'the true constituent units of a myth are not the isolated relations but *bundles of such relations* and it is only as bundles that these relations can be put to use and combined so as to produce meaning' (Lévi-Strauss 1955, p. 431). The idea of 'bundles of relations' is key not only to Lévi-Strauss's argument but also to the wider concepts we are exploring here. The potential relations between all of the elements involved in a musical create an intricate web of interwoven layers of codes and interpretations, creating bundles of potential meaning. Susan Melrose also considers a dramatic work to contain 'a bundle of semiotic potential, held together by the differing energetic input of group members' (Melrose 1994, p. 221). The idea of 'semiotic potential' is important in recognizing the many layers of meaning and interpretation which might be there in the musical.

The musicologist Kofi Agawu (whose work we will return to in Section Two) explores the concept of semiotics, thematic material and referential methods in *Playing with Signs* (1991). Agawu's approach in his book considers the way that units of musical material have functions. He isn't talking about musical theatre, but rather music in the Western classical tradition. However, we can see the relevance to thinking of music in musical theatre. In the context of music being used as a storytelling tool to convey narrative, to apply the idea of functions to performance modes, as well as to narrative, would seem a logical extension. The score of a musical contains a high level of narrative impulse, an impulse which is then specified with more certainty in the interrelations between the music itself and the lyrics of the songs. The prevalence of underscore and dance material in the genre of musical theatre also strongly contributes to the score containing its own musical signs which work both independently from, and in collaboration with, the libretto. Indeed, the creation of a difference in the meaning connoted by the musical sign and by the lyrical sign is a compositional technique used to create 'bundles of relations' and multiple signs. As we have implied already, musical material can be conceived of on different levels; from small-scale gestural phrases or musical motifs, to characteristics relating to a high level notion of musical style.

Agawu also discusses the notions of *introversive* and *extroversive* semiosis. Introversive semiosis is the idea that a sign is created within the original material – for example when a link is made between a character or event and the music that we hear at that time within the musical. Extroversive semiosis is when we hear a unit of music which carries meaning from *outside* the world of the show – i.e. from the 'real world'.

The idea of extroversive semiosis has a long history in classical musical, and Agawu particularly uses the term 'topic' to refer to such signifying gestures in music of the eighteenth and nineteenth centuries. Agawu's various lists of topics show that the scale of gesture can vary significantly, from a small motif or musical cell (e.g. a hunting call) to a complete style (such as learned style) or indeed form (such as gavotte). We have already looked at musical theatre equivalents of some of these examples – small cellular units of musical material, and the idea of a style carrying associations with it. We will be looking at equivalent forms in Section Two when we look at song structures.

Exploration of themes

Keeping the language of themes, motifs and cells in mind let's go back to the examples of new musicals from Chapter 1 and explore how some of these ideas, alongside that of semiotics, might relate to those briefs.

A reminder of the first show brief:

Show's concept: set against a backdrop of a fictionalized city where industry has dried up.

Essence of the score: the score draws on the soundworld of colliery bands as a starting point, exploring their timbre, harmonic language and textures.

The universal theme for this show is about reclaiming joy. Its main themes portray the opposite of that universal theme: the elements which supress joy. This is an example which shows that themes are not necessarily subtopics of the universal theme, but rather relate to it in some way, shape or form: in this instance by standing in opposition to it. The impetus of the show becomes about overcoming each of the themes of repression and suppression to finally arrive at the rebirth of joy. The colliery band soundworld can be seen as an extroversive reference in solidarity with places that have experienced an industry, such as mining (the word colliery relates to coal mining), disappearing. The brass band sound, alongside a particular style of music, acts semiotically as a signifier for this extroversive reference. Within the score are foundations of a variety of dance rhythms (mostly ballroom) to signify subliminally a joy that bubbles beneath the surface and cannot be repressed forever.

The second brief we saw was as below:

Show's concept: a show all about the natural world and its cycle, with a view to righting the disharmony of the Earth.

Essence of the score: the score reflects the mathematical patterns found in nature, for example using the Fibonacci sequence as a compositional tool.

The universal theme of this show is about stewardship of our planet and working in harmony with it. We discussed previously that there might be a way into this score using numerical techniques involving the numbers that are found occurring in the natural world. This implies a potential cellular and motivic score, where the music is constructed from small building blocks. In terms of themes, the show is episodic, involving interactions with different forms of the planet's landscape. Thematic material could revolve around the different landscapes, with different themes constructed from small cells for each landscape. Alternatively, ideas could be grouped thematically along the lines of qualities of relations with the planet – for example main themes might involve attitudes such as battling, leeching, destruction and then the positive opposites of these negative approaches. In either instance, the use of small-scale cells and building from those, as opposed to sweeping long-line melodies, might be more in keeping with the dramaturgy of the piece. Semiotics may operate in a more introversive way whereby cells within the show create associated meaning which carries through in development of the motifs in the show.

Our third and final brief was as follows:

> **Show's concept:** a traditional Christmas pantomime involving an adapted fairy tale and typical good versus evil tropes.
>
> **Essence of the score:** each of the characters has their own theme based on their particular 'I want'. These musical themes are then developed, modified and carried through the rest of the show.

This is the show for which we discussed the leitmotif model previously. The universal theme for this show is about good winning the day, in a fairly traditional way. The style of the piece is bold and comical, and navigation through the themes is most appropriate through a process of clear character identification. The main themes of this show arise from the various means by which good fights evil, and as is often the way in pantomime, these strands are closely aligned to individual characters. Other related themes are constructed by exploring the trajectory of a particular character, or group of characters, and using small motifs from key songs to develop further material for their other related songs. Often in such shows, each character has a strong sense of forward plan that they are attempting to carry out, and so themes become indicative of the means by which that larger-scale plan is being unravelled. Pantomime is likely to involve extroversive semiosis, with musical references to styles and semiotic associations outside of the world of the pantomime itself. Panto is also a self-referent form of theatre, whereby there are types of set pieces that have developed over centuries of the form. This is also a form of semiosis, whereby the show is referring to associations with its own form. Musical examples of this might be the drum fill and cymbal crash that has become associated with a punch line joke in pantomime, or the three-chord doom-filled progression that has come to mean the entrance of the baddie. Thematic development along character lines in the show might also involve reference to soundworlds from outside the show, but may also in turn become a strong form of introversive semiosis whereby the leitmotif for a character becomes infused with meaning regarding their 'good' or 'evil' status.

Let's now continue the discussion of themes and semiotic signs through consideration of some of the musicals from the canon that we are looking at in Part One.

In *Billy Elliot,* the universal theme of **identity** can be seen as portrayed throughout the musical by the musical styles utilized at any one time. There are stylistic strands that interweave throughout the musical, each of which is related to a theme of the story.

The theme of **dancing** often draws on extroversive references to the world of 'show business'. This can be seen in the numbers 'Shine' (when Mrs Wilkinson's ballet class is first introduced and tropes of Golden Age Broadway show styles are drawn upon), 'Expressing Yourself' (when Michael's expressiveness conjures a whole fantasy show sequence complete with sparkling curtain and giant dancing dresses) and 'Born to Boogie' (in which boogie woogie tropes are drawn on, amongst other dance and show-style tropes, for Mrs Wilkinson, Billy and Mr Braithwaite to move through the stages of preparation for Billy's audition for the Royal Ballet School). This strand can be seen as related to Billy's discovery of his talent for dancing, and Mrs Wilkinson's realization of the potential future that could lie ahead of him. The inclusion of Michael in this musical strand is important as another ally for Billy; his friend who plays an important part in his resolve to lean into his true identity. Another ally for Billy is his grandma, and 'Grandma's Song' sits alongside the musical thematic strand of dancing. As Grandma tells Billy of how awful her husband was, the moments when they felt connection were when they were dancing. In keeping with her character and the time period when this would have occurred, the musical trope here is one of waltzes and it is in this genre that Grandma sits within the dancing tropes of the show, rather than in the glitzy show style of Michael and Mrs Wilkinson.

The theme of **mining** plays in contrast to the theme of **dancing**, and its strand of songs draw on tropes of protest songs and marching styles; songs that make use of homophonic textures of choral harmony. These songs can be seen at key structural moments in the show: the opening song 'The Stars Look Down', the beginning of Act 2 'Merry Christmas Mrs Thatcher' and near the end of the show 'Once We Were Kings'. *Billy Elliot* tells the story of an individual set against the vital backdrop of the miners' strike in the era of Mrs Thatcher being prime minister. The culture surrounding the mines and the immediate mining familial context for Billy is crucial to his sense of identity: he is essentially torn between the two cultures throughout the show, and the binary musical styles help to demonstrate this in the score.

It is in 'Solidarity' that these strands of identity come up against each other in direct juxtaposition. Billy's two worlds interact with each other choreographically and musically as the ballet class and the strikes happen simultaneously. Musically, 'Solidarity' mostly inhabits the world of the miners in style drawing on similar tropes and techniques as are found in the other miners' songs. Choreographically, the song fuses the rigidity of the line up of policemen with the fluidity of the ballet class. Billy, often, is physically caught between the two. Musically, the world of the miners is dominant at this point, as is the case dramatically with this moment being Billy's first explorations in dance, without the notion that he could leave his familial world and explore his vocation. The singing of the main chorus structure by the ballet girls of Billy's class demonstrates the crossover of the ballet class into the world of the strikes, in the same way that choreographically the policemen detachedly take on the role of partnering the ballet dancers in their class. The two worlds fuse and combine, symbolic of the two worlds residing within Billy and the choice of identity that he needs to make in the show. In 'Angry Dance', parts of 'Solidarity' return musically, and the thematic idea of the protests intermingling with the world of dance is notched up a level of intensity. Here, Billy's dance world is much more aggressive, expressing his anger and upset at being forbidden from dancing, while the protests have escalated to riots. It is in this guise that the riot gear of the policemen forms a literal barricade to Billy dancing, blocking him from progressing in his path. Again, the musical world of the miners is dominant and this ending of Act 1 leaves us in no doubt that the world of dance is being shut out for Billy, demonstrated both musically and physically. Musically, the thematic strand of dancing finds its full expression in a truly extroversive reference – the 'Swan Lake' section. Here, a section of Tchaikovsky's score from the ballet is used for Billy to dance to, mirrored by a grown-up version of himself. This is not an extroversive reference in the sense of drawing on tropes, characteristics and ideas, but rather a literal quotation from one of the most familiar ballet scores. This quotation of material stands out as a reference to the real world outside of the show. In this moment, the rock-based soundworld of the protests is lost altogether, and the score foreshadows the fullness of the identity that will play out for Billy in the future.

The third thematic strand in the show might be seen as one of guiding influence, and that is the strand relating to Billy's **parents**. This is mostly expressed through the letters, sung between Billy's Mum and himself in 'The Letter (Mum's Letter)' and 'The Letter (Billy's Reply)' which share musical similarity. This thematic strand is written in a gentle, balladic style, demonstrating loving compassion and the encouragement of Billy's mum for him to be himself as he grows up. This thematic strand can be seen to mediate between the two worlds of mining and dance, and helps Billy to navigate between the two. She was of his familial (mining) environment, but she encourages him towards the world of ballet, given that that is his gift. This trope is taken up by Jackie in 'He Could Be a Star' in which he breaks down into the gentle, simple balladic style, amidst the turmoil of the rest of the sequence. By taking on more of the musical style of Billy's Mum, his Dad is able to make the transition into supporting Billy in his chosen identity, as his Mum would do. Billy locks into this style at the beginning of 'Electricity'. While this becomes a much bigger and showy number, its beginnings are rooted in the soundworld of emotional truth, initially established in the show by his Mum.

It can be seen that the three strands of musical soundworld help to navigate through the universal theme of identity: one broad musical strand for each identity, and a third that helps to mediate between the two. This is a way of creating thematic worlds which mostly focus on style as the umbrella for each strand: a broadly rock-inspired world of protest songs and marches; a soundworld of show style and other dance tropes; and one of simple, emotive ballad.

Jason Robert Brown's *The Last Five Years* is a musical about the breakdown of a relationship, both characters telling the same story as Cathy moves backwards in chronological time and Jamie moves forward. As, arguably, a concept musical, the universal theme, as we have stated previously is about the breakdown of a relationship. The themes which emanate from that therefore take on the various aspects of what has contributed to their relationship's story, and their own activities and characteristics. The elements of this could be seen as Jamie's book writing career taking over, Jamie's wandering eye, Cathy's insecurities and Cathy's struggling career as a performer. It is not the case that each of these elements has their own musical strand in a neat and tidy way. However, there are stylistic and thematic strands in the musical which lead to a sense of both shared, and separated and contrasted worlds. As with *Billy Elliot*, there is a sense of the traditional Golden Age musical soundworld being used as an extroversive reference, to represent Cathy's performing career, and the insecurities that are attached to that. This is first fully heard through the style of the song 'A Summer in Ohio', while Cathy is away there on a job. It is in 'A Miracle Would Happen/When You Are Home' that the style takes on its complete crossover between diegesis and Cathy's feelings about Jamie. As Cathy's plot is telling the story backwards, we hear the working out of 'When You Are Home' before we hear its use in the diegetic context of her audition piece in 'Climbing Uphill'. The song draws on the tropes associated with protagonists of bygone eras when the female might play more of a subservient role, waiting for her male counterpart. This trope is set into relief in the parallels in Cathy's life as she waits for a very absent Jamie to come home, while the audience know he is unfaithful at this point in their story. The extroversive reference of this style subtly draws associations between the reference and the character of Cathy. In 'Climbing Uphill' the song in the audition is set in contrast with the heavier, folk/musical theatre style of Cathy's frustrations about her life attending audition after audition. The 'When You Are Home' theme then takes on a further variation later in the 'Climbing Uphill' sequence as Cathy sings her inner monologue to the tune of the audition song that she is once again singing. Fitting many more syllables in than the tune is written for, the musical theme takes on a commentary on itself as we imagine the image that Cathy is portraying to the panel at the audition while the audience is privy to her inner thoughts.

There are further extroversive references in the show, such as the classical string interlude three-quarters of the way through 'Still Hurting'. This draws on the trope of classical string quartets generally, set in the midst of Cathy's powerful opening emotive ballad, but more specifically than this, the lines shape the general contour of the opening of Bach's 'Jesu Joy of Man's Desiring'. This is not a direct quote or reference, but the shape is there such that this popular wedding theme is juxtaposed with the complete breakdown of the marriage that Cathy is expressing. Not only is the world of the classical wedding quartet being alluded to in instrumentation, but also specifically in the contours of the material at this point. In the film version of the musical, this theme comes back at the beginning of 'See I'm Smiling', picking up Cathy's strand of the story, having been alternated with Jamie at the beginning of their relationship. In this instance, the 'Jesu Joy'–inspired material cadences into a new riff, becoming the new bedrock of the song that is to come. This reference back to the wedding-esque material in 'Still Hurting' aids the clues at the beginning of the musical that Jamie and Cathy are in different time zones, and so having moved out of Jamie's first song, we are taken forward to where Cathy is, at the end of their story.

There is some shared material between Jamie and Cathy. While 'The Next Ten Minutes' is the only song in which their time worlds coincide, there are moments of shared musical material between songs. The clearest example of this is in the middle of 'Moving Too Fast' where Jamie moves into a bridge section which is a re-imagined version of Cathy's melody in 'Still Hurting'. This is not a reprise – it is not long enough for that – but rather a recontextualization of material which takes on a new kind of meaning. This is an example of introversive semiosis – where the show creates meaning attached to a musical theme, and then draws on this established meaning, often then slightly shifting it or providing new information on it. In this case, Jamie is still in the excitable first stages after their meeting, but he is also indicating that he is aware that in all sense their relationship is moving too fast. The recontextualization of the material from 'Still Hurting', the most painful moment in the songs of Cathy's journey, recalls the fact that they are indeed moving too fast and that this story will end in the pain of the separation that we have already seen. As song number four in the show, this continues to establish the time rules of the show, as it is still relatively early in the musical, making musical thematic links for the audience. The melody from 'Still Hurting' has been established semiotically as a sign for emotional pain, and that sign is what is being drawn on here.

Summing up

We have seen here multiple ways of how the features of the score can arise from consideration of the dramatic universal and main themes, and how part of the job of the composer, in collaboration and discussion with the rest of the team, is to 'translate' these ideas into music. We have seen how these themes can arise out of the narrative of the piece, but we have also seen instances where thematic material arises from character; their character traits and motives in the show in the context of the plot. And so, our next chapter will focus on shared language and tools in the creation of music born out of character.

3

Theme, character and musical parameters

We are going to turn now to the question of character, and how considerations of the personalities of your characters may help to determine the various qualities of their musical soundworlds. In this chapter we will be looking at the concept of 'efforts' as created by Rudolph Laban to see how this can help to determine character. We will also be breaking down the composites of 'music' into its various elements and naming each individually so that we can think about the score on a detailed level, element by element.

Laban efforts

The language of **Laban efforts** may be familiar to those who have studied physical performance: they have long been used as a choreographic tool for dancers – as was choreographer and dance artist Rudolf Laban's initial impetus when he created the method – but the efforts have also been applied widely to the actor in development of the physicality of their character. I would like to take this long-established practice a step further and apply the same conceptualization to the *music* of a character. The language of Laban efforts is inherently musical, speaking of inner rhythms and tempi. Music and movement share the characteristics of occurring through time and space and having their own sense of flow and weight: the language of Laban efforts aids this shared sense of flow and can be utilized to great effect regarding the creation of the musical language of a character, and the musical language of a dramatic situation.

The efforts are built around different qualities being given to: time, space and weight. **Time** is characterized as quick or sustained; movement through **space** as approached directly or indirectly and with either a heavy or a light quality of **weight**. The respective combinations of these three parameters result in the names that are attributed to each of the eight combinations of 'efforts':

	Time	Space	Weight
Punch	Quick	Direct	Heavy
Slash	Quick	Indirect	Heavy
Dab	Quick	Direct	Light
Flick	Quick	Indirect	Light
Press	Sustained	Direct	Heavy
Wring	Sustained	Indirect	Heavy
Glide	Sustained	Direct	Light
Float	Sustained	Indirect	Light

Let's take a look at this in practice. In the song 'See I'm Smiling' in the film version of *The Last Five Years*, Anna Kendrick (who plays Cathy) has physical movement that can be seen as light through the first half of the song. She maintains stillness for short periods, and then has little sudden movements that are indirect – reflective of the awkwardness between herself and Jamie in this moment, as they try and work their way through this exchange together. It might be said that her movements alternate between glide – light, sustained and direct – and flick – light, quick and indirect. The small sudden flick moments demonstrate the awkwardness amidst a certain degree of peace between them portrayed by the glide effort.

But what does this have to do with music? These same efforts can be extended to think about the music for the song as well. Let's look further at

'See I'm Smiling' and we can find those same characteristics of glide and flick in the music itself. Each phrase of the verse starts with a little sudden upbeat, proceeding into a fairly short phrase with the end of the motifs often ending in a small upward inflection. In these ways, each of these short phrases can be seen as synonymous with the 'flick' effort. In the chorus, and indeed the bridge, the music becomes much more aligned with the 'glide' effort. The beginning of the chorus has an octave leap – a direct jump – followed by a descent. This pattern of a direct intervallic leap followed by a descent recurs through the verse. The phrases are longer and more sustained. Overall, these patterns indicate a melody that is light, direct and sustained, invoking the 'glide' effort. The accompaniment of the verse at the start of the song gives a different sense of effort: that of 'dab'. There are individual pairs of repeated short notes that are more in keeping with quick, direct, light sense of 'dab', allowing an easing into the singing which leans into the sense of awkwardness, over which the vocal can operate. This changes in the second verse and the rolling sense of accompaniment becomes much more sustained, leaning into the sense of 'glide'.

However, this is a song of two halves dramatically. As Cathy realizes that Jamie won't be staying for very long, her emotional state completely changes and so does the musical effort. The accompanimental patterns turn to heavier, short stabs which align with the effort 'punch' – heavy, direct and quick. Cathy's vocal line is more sustained in the way that the words tumble out than the 'punch' effort might indicate, but the flow of words serves the purpose of propelling her towards multiple 'punched' words and it can be seen that this effort applies to her vocals in this section as well.

Musical components

A character's storytelling in song happens way before any lyrics are sung. Lyrics, of course, are vital in giving specificity to storytelling, but the music itself is also telling a story. Not only that, but the musical itself may also be telling several layers of a story, stacked within the various faces of the components of the music.

It's time to start looking at more musical specifics. When either analysing or conceptualizing music in the composition process, it can be helpful to break it down into its component parts in order to take each element separately and think about its particular characteristics:

- Tempo – the speed of the music;

- Rhythm – the way the beat is subdivided and the approach to that;

- Melody – the way that pitches occurring one after the other create a tune or line as if they were the equivalent of words placed one after the other creating a sentence;

- Harmony – the notes that happen at the same time create types of chords which is called the harmonic language;

- Texture – the way that parts move together carries different effect and storytelling potential – e.g. lines that occur in the same rhythm but at different pitches (homophonic texture) creates a chordal approach as opposed to separate lines overlapping and interweaving with each other (polyphonic texture);

- Accompaniment figures – what is happening in the piano part or band should be thought of as telling its own story, as well as the way in which it relates to the vocal lines;

- Orchestration and timbre – the particular instruments and voices chosen at any one moment (orchestration) create certain types of resonance with certain qualities of sound (timbre).

Each one of these layers can be thought of as having its own dramatic potential, as well as the story that can be implied through the ways they are combined together. It can be helpful to think of these elements as some being 'horizontal' and some being 'vertical'. This essentially originates from what musical notation looks like when scored – elements that move through time (melody, rhythm) are read left to right like a book (i.e. horizontally) whereas components that come together in any one moment (harmony, accompanimental figures, texture, orchestration) are stacked on top of each other (i.e. vertical).

Horizontal elements: Rhythm and tempo

The horizontal elements of rhythm and tempo both relate to the use of time in music, and the way that time is subdivided into units. We can think of this concept in relation to tempo – the overall speed of the music – as well as specific rhythm – the way that time is subdivided. In the same way that Laban efforts encourage consideration of characterization through a person's innate tempo, this too can be considered when writing songs for each particular character: what do their predominant characteristics suggest about their use of time? Are they slow to respond, or stuck around the same thought loops which might suggest a slow natural character tempo? Do they exhibit a nervous use of energy which might result in a faster character tempo? In a similar way, we can then be more specific about a character's use of rhythm, and how they might be represented as a character through the way that metre is subdivided. The slow and steady character we first considered may also have a regular use of metre, measuring out each bar in a regular and consistent way. However, they may be slow to respond but actually what happens internally in their mind is a series of unstructured thoughts which are anything but regular. In this instance the composer might decide to represent the speed of response through tempo, but for the scattered thought process to be born out through irregular use of rhythm. Alternatively, irregularity of rhythm may also represent an ease and a natural everyday quality.

In 'Changing My Major to Joan', from *Fun Home*, the changes in tempo and rhythm of the vocal line throughout the song do exactly this job of portraying Alison's various states of mind as they evolve. To begin with the vocal line is slowly paced; tentative. This speeds up with freedom brought about through the triplet rhythm as Alison's thoughts spiral thinking about the previous night. As she begins to recount the events of the night before, Alison's rhythm is almost entirely regular quavers. In another context, this might indicate a well-thought through or factual character, but in Alison's context at this point the incessant regularity, barely pausing for breath, shows her thoughts flooding her mind without relenting. It is the change of metre to 3/4 that allows her thought process to slow down a little, and Alison gives a more measured response to her feelings for Joan. Only a little though. The choice of 3/4 metre here allows for the feeling of one in a bar which can create an impression of being caught up in a whirlwind going round and round, which by the second time the chorus appears is exactly what happens. The two techniques of conversational rhythm, versus the waltz feel are used in alternation through the song to chart Alison's emotional journey. In the middle section, as she expresses her fear, the rhythm feels incredibly free (although in fact all notated precisely) until she states that she is scared, the word on which she sings one of the most sustained notes rhythmically in the song. As she crescendos through this sustain, it seems to allow her to break out of the patter rhythm and return to a more resolute, solid and slower 4/4, grounding her before the final waltz time. This song demonstrates how rhythm can be integral to storytelling and allow the character to go on a journey musically solely through the use of changing time signatures, rhythm and tempi.

The composer may decide to use irregular rhythms to demonstrate natural speech quality, without making the music 'feel' irregular – it simply moves along at the rhythm that it would if the character were speaking. This technique is particularly relevant to verbatim techniques, where music is written to exactly reflect the natural speech rhythm. An example of a musical that is entirely based around this technique is *London Road*. In *London Road* at times irregularity of rhythm will suggest a natural speech quality. *However*, in musicalizing every single element of the natural speech what results interestingly is something incredibly stylized which is pointedly angular in its rhythmic quality and makes the characters feel stilted at times. It is interesting that complete faithfulness to natural speech quality does not always result in the impression of naturalness when singing.

Horizontal elements: Melody

The manner in which pitches are placed one by one next to each other to create melody might be likened to Laban's category of 'space'. Melody is a form of placing resonant frequencies in space and the movement from one to the other creates a sense of line; singing a melody could be seen as if you were almost drawing a shape through the air with your voice. It can be imagined that singing the same pitch one after the other would create the image of a straight horizontal line which might be likened to the 'direct' quality of half of the Laban efforts, whereas a melody that involved jumping with large intervals between each pitch might be considered 'indirect'. A character can be imagined who is certain of what they have to say and whose melodies might therefore move in more direct lines, using step-wise, scalic movement or indeed direct octave leaps, whereas a character who is fumbling about for an answer might sing a melody which meanders around pitch grouping with a more indirect use of melodic line.

This is exactly what happens in 'Changing My Major to Joan'. Alison's vocal line is very restricted and lacking in a linear sense of direction, particularly in the verses. In combination with the approach to rhythm and metre discussed above, the melody further enables the sense of the character going round in circles and without a sense of clear direction. It is as if these verses function melodically in a similar way to the operatic technique of recitative: a rhythmic form of singing with reduced melodic expansion that allows for focus to be on the detail of the words. In the waltz choruses in 'Changing My Major' there is a little more of a sense of linear direction and shape to the melodic lines, creating more of a sense of phrase than was found in the verse. However, the pitch grouping is still quite restricted in range initially, but grows gradually through the song as Alison finds an expansion of freedom and expression.

Vertical elements: Texture, accompaniment, orchestration and timbre

Texture, accompanimental patterns, orchestration and thereby timbre are all contributing factors to, what might be considered, the 'weight' category of Laban's efforts. Decisions made regarding the use of the instruments' range, choosing certain instruments for their quality of sound and how many instruments or voices are singing or playing at once and using what kind of texture all contribute to the heaviness or lightness of the weight of the musical score. Music is highly codified in our culture; for example, certain sonorities have automatic associations for the listener – at its simplest, a deep sonorous sound at the low end of the piano keyboard might indicate a heavier quality to a delicate light sound in the top range of the instrument (the range of an instrument is referred to as its tessitura). This is compounded all the more by the different sonorities given by making the low sound that of a brass instrument such as a tuba, and the lighter note being played with the airier quality of a flute. This is highly simplistic and does not give acknowledgement to the vast variety of characteristic which can be attained on each individual instrument, but you understand the basic point being made. It's all a matter of deliberate choice according to what you want your character or narrative unit to *feel* like.

'Edges of the World' from *Fun Home* demonstrates how orchestration can be used to storytelling effect. In this song Bruce's inner world deteriorates until he stands in front of a moving truck. The recitative section at the beginning of the song features piano notes being played quickly without a sense of tempo or pulse, alongside sliding high violin lines, also with a sense of randomness. Bruce is singing in a measured time, in metre, while the orchestration portrays this sense of time has been broken and a lack of control going on underneath. In the short interlude after the recitative, high-sounding instruments are used – glockenspiel and high violin lines. These are replaced in the first verse by sonorous instruments with the prevalence of strings, and bassoon along with piano. There is a change again in the slower, placid section which is lighter with largely piano and acoustic guitar. In the second verse, the orchestration starts to change with the addition of sudden, short drum bursts and the high harmonic violin lines, recalling the randomness of the beginning. As Bruce becomes more distressed, these dissonant elements of the orchestration increase. The sudden change to the slow, placid section hails an equally sudden change in orchestration back to the simple piano and picked guitar with lush solo clarinet and string lines. In the recitative section that follows, the orchestration is stripped right back to a sustained drone, gradually building in texture until the tremolo and extended string textures of the agitated section. The orchestration continues to swell now across all ranges of sonority covering a wide spectrum of full ensemble until the truck horn takes over from the instruments.

It is important within this category of orchestration to consider the timbre of *voice*. Specific voice types have long held codified meanings within musico-dramatic forms: there is a long tradition of the tenor voice (high male voice type) being used for leading male heroic roles in the world of opera for example. These can become stereotyped, but it is certainly the case that different voice types and ranges convey different qualities of timbre which imply certain qualities to the character. A strong example of this is seen in *Hadestown*. The character of Orpheus is introduced by Hermes as being a special and unique kind of person, like no other, with an affinity with the gods. Orpheus's voice and musical language is crucial in the show due to the saving song that he is creating. The part is written for a countertenor voice – that is a male voice singing in the range of a contralto – and as such, Orpheus often sings with a falsetto quality. There is a tradition of this vocal quality having associations with purity, and with an ethereal otherworldliness. The dramatic situation that Orpheus finds himself in makes sense of these associations. It also sets Orpheus apart from the other male characters in the show vocally, in alignment with Hermes's insistence that he is unique. At the other end of the timbre spectrum, Hades is played by a performer with a very low bass voice – a basso profundo. It is so low, that the vocal line is not always directly pitched, meaning that there is a pronounced impression of timbre rather than pitch in several scenarios. Hades is the God of the Underworld, and the extremity of his voice gives further character to the idea of the extreme underground depths of the Underworld. When the two characters, Orpheus and Hades, go up against each other and Orpheus's fate lies in the hands of Hades, the vocal extremities between the two voice types are as far apart as they could be. This is dramatically helpful and is symbolic of their inhabiting different worlds, but also the difference in their timbres gives strong messages regarding character: one with an ethereal quality, and one with an extreme earthiness to the voice.

Vertical elements: Harmony

Continuing with the idea of music being codified, such is the case for the harmonic language of a score. A combination of centuries of musical history and the ways we respond naturally to the consonance and dissonance created by placing particular pitches in combination with each other mean that we naturally ascribe a certain feel to whether chords sound like they belong together or otherwise. As a storytelling tool, these codes can be of great advantage to indicate impressions of tranquillity, a sense of something gelling, or unease and a generic feeling that something is 'not right'. Just as we noted that the horizontal selection and placing of pitches in melody can be imagined within the Laban efforts context of 'space', so is the case for the vertical placing of pitches in harmony: a bare fifth may give a more 'direct' impression than a dissonant or added chord which may feel more 'indirect' for example. While harmony is discussed here in vertical terms, of course the moving from one moment of harmony to another brings in a horizontal aspect and this movement in itself creates a new story: while one chord in isolation may be consonant, its progression to the next may feel unexpected – outside the realms of traditional functional harmony – or predictable and bring about a comforting familiarity. So, while a bare fifth on its own may feel direct, context may alter this view if it continues on to unfamiliar harmonic pastures.

Continuing to explore the earlier example of 'Edges of the World' from *Fun Home*, harmony and tonality can be seen to play a very important role in the storytelling of Bruce's distress. The song starts in B major, but there is no strong sense of this tonality at all. The piano pattern that is indicated to be playing without a sense of metre sketches out an arpeggio figure in the right hand which spans broadly from tonic to dominant, and one in the left which simultaneously sketches out dominant to tonic. However, due to the random effect created in this section there is not a strong sense of the B major nature of the start of the song. This allows for a strong sense of landing in the first metred section – the verse – which is in F minor. However, it doesn't actually cadence into a strong sense of F minor for the interlude in between – this sense of arrival comes with the vocal in the vocal entry in the verse. The verse then repeats a sequence of Fm(add9) – Gb(#4) – Ebm7. The use of the move up to flat 2 to the Gb chord, moving up just a minor second, gives a certain sense of eeriness, particularly with the added note of #4 in the second chord. Tonality changes again for the slow, placid section, moving down to Eb major. This shifts again as Bruce becomes more and more agitated, to Gb, and then down to F major, before moving to G major literally for the final sustained note leading to the truck horn. The tonality of the song is restless and it moves far away from the B major tonality sketched out in the opening recitative. Throughout the song, the tonal centres move from F minor to Eb major, then Gb major, F major, G major. Each shift here is not very far in terms of the moving of tonic bass note, but they are large shifts in terms of cycles of closely related keys – they are not expected modulations. This restlessness plays a large part in the musical storytelling of Bruce's loss of control and his breaking down into more and more distress.

Laban efforts and music

If we return to the original Laban efforts, and consider how musical elements might map against this, here are some ideas as initial starting points. Of course, there are myriad possibilities for how the musical parameters might be combined to show the characteristics you are wanting, but here are some initial ideas as a starting point:

	Time	Space	Weight	Possible musical elements
Punch	Quick	Direct	Heavy	Tempo: Slow enough to give the heaviness necessary Rhythm: Sudden stabs to give the *punch* pace, but within the context of a moderate overall tempo. Measured. Melody: Direct movement between pitches Harmony: Consonant Texture: Chordal, homophonic Accompaniment: Chordal Timbre: Lower registers somewhere in the mix for heaviness.
Slash	Quick	Indirect	Heavy	The difference here from *punch* is the indirect use of space. This might be achieved through use of wider interval leaps in the melody, or perhaps by a more unexpected approach to harmony.

	Time	**Space**	**Weight**	**Possible musical elements**
Dab	Quick	Direct	Light	Different to *punch* in the lightness of weight which might be achieved through a lighter texture, a higher tessitura range, a more delicate use of orchestration or approach to accompanimental pattern or texture. Due to its lightness, the quickness of time could be approached by a faster tempo overall as the lightness gives a nimbleness that enables speed. This combination of quick time and light weight may result in a more involved accompaniment pattern involving more figuration but still maintaining a 'direct' approach to space in this regard (this may, for example, mean it is still fairly chordal).
Flick	Quick	Indirect	Light	Similar to *dab* but with an indirect approach to space which could be conveyed, for example, by interweaving textures in the accompaniment or vocal parts, but maintaining a flicking quality to this polyphony.
Press	Sustained	Direct	Heavy	As with *punch* except with a sustained approach to time, perhaps resulting in longer note values, growing in dynamic through sustained notes, use of instrumentation which can be sustained, or through increased use of the sustain pedal for a piano reduction.
Wring	Sustained	Indirect	Heavy	Similar to techniques of *press* but with an indirect use of space, perhaps brought about through approaches to melody or harmonic language.
Glide	Sustained	Direct	Light	Different from *press* in the lightness of weight which might be achieved through tessitura, articulation and instrumentation differences.

	Time	**Space**	**Weight**	**Possible musical elements**
Float	Sustained	Indirect	Light	Similar to *flick* but with a sustained approach to time. This may result in longer note values in the rhythm, and a sense of connectedness in melodic writing. The indirectness might be achieved through intervals in the melody, through unexpected harmony or through interweaving textures which can in themselves also be more sustained in their polyphony in this effort, as opposed to in those efforts which have a quick approach to time.

Let's have a look at some examples as viewed from the perspective of considering the Laban efforts and the elements of music all together to see how character can be portrayed through the composing choices made in the musicals *Six* and *London Road*.

Laban efforts and music in practice

In the musical *Six*, the opening of 'Ex-Wives' is characterized by hits over a soft low drone. The hits continue into the song proper, with use of stop time – short stabs, deconstructing the *Greensleeves* melody popularly associated with Henry VIII – with two bars of instrumental silence for the unaccompanied vocal lines in between hits. This establishes a clear *punch* effort to the song, and indeed to the show as a whole given this is its opening. *Six* has become known for many as a symbol of female empowerment, and the use of the strong *punch* effort in the music is part of how this is conveyed. It is an effort that runs throughout many of the songs: stop time is used at the start of 'No Way' with similar stabs to those found in 'Ex-Wives' and the sporadic punch-like use of the bass line in the verses continues this feel; the same technique is used at the beginning of 'Don't Lose Ur Head' and again, throughout the verses; in a different way it can be seen in the character of the rising bass line in the verses of 'Get Down' with each individual note being a discreet *punch*; and it also features in specific moments of 'I Don't Need Your Love' with stop time being used when the song takes on more feminist features. These examples are based on rhythmic interpretations of the effort *punch* but it can be seen in a context of timbre as well. The timbre – the sound quality of the instruments and vocals used – could be said to often also invoke the *punch* effort in *Six* through the very strong, hard-hitting kick drum sound and certain specific electronic bass sounds which can be characterized as heavy, direct and quick. Elements of *punch* are seen in this interpretation of it in songs which primarily feature other efforts, such as 'Heart of Stone' where, in that instance, it is the emphasized snare sound that gives a sense of *punch* amidst the other efforts discussed below.

We've seen that the *punch* effort is used to unify all of the six wives together with an overriding sense of strength, but *Six* is a good example of how the differences in the characters can be seen in the music, through the lens of Laban efforts. The premise of *Six* is that the women are trying to ascertain who had the toughest time married to Henry VIII; therefore from the outset they establish themselves as different from each other and the very point is that they are *not* simply a collection of wives characterized only by their link of being married to Henry – they each have their own story. This is well-known to be demonstrated through evoking links to different musical styles through similarities with individual pop artists, but if we drill that down to the characteristics of the music itself and analyse this through the framework of efforts, it gives a sense of *how* in broad terms they are being characterized through the music. We said that in 'Heart of Stone' there are elements of *punch* going on amidst other efforts. This indicates that we can conceive of this idea in layers – different layers of the music may well be giving different cues and indications which amalgamate together to create a three-dimensional view of the character. In musicals, it is not always (or perhaps even not often) desirable that the lyrics and the music are conveying exactly the same message. Part of the strength of the musical theatre form comes in the totality of a composite message – multiple layers of meaning joining together from different aural and visual cues that gives a rounded and multi-dimensional story. Layers of subtext can be created through the music and lyrics giving slightly different aspects of a situation, while visual elements – such as the staging, scenographic elements and lighting – will be telling their own part of the story as well. Some of these will overlap and reinforce each other, whereas some of it will be discreet to one of the specific elements in the whole. This same principle can be applied to music itself. Music can be seen in layers – it can be visually helpful to note that this can be seen in the simultaneous horizontal and vertical reading of a manuscript score where multiple lines of staves are being read at the same time, as if each stave is one part of a big layer cake. It is a good rule of thumb when composing and arranging to try and not have more than three dominant factors going on at any one time. Even in large orchestrations, sections of the orchestra will be working together in order to not overwhelm with the possible confusion of too many elements going on at the same time. While this 'three' could be thought of in various ways, let's think of this in a simple three-part structure of what the rhythm section is doing (thinking of this as the 'bottom' of our layer cake), a middle texture (often in this context keys, synths or guitars) and a top line (usually in this context this will be the vocals). If we return to the first sections of 'Ex-Wives' applying this layer idea, we can see that the rhythm section and middle are both using *punch* but that in fact the top layer of the vocals is not. The vocals are much more sustained here, and while there might be an element of *punch* in the way the actor emphasizes the performance quality of the vocals, the melody line itself is not quite one of punching. If we turn to the verse of the song, the vocal line is certainly still heavy, but the shape of the vocal line indicates an indirectness rather than the directness of *punch*, and the use of time is sustained in that there is no rhythmic air in between notes – the vocal line is legato. This suggests that the vocal line of the verse has more of a *wring* effort to it, while the instrumentals are still in *punch*.

Six is a show in which each of Henry VIII's six wives are able to put their story forward, and therefore there is a structure where they each have a song that encapsulates the characteristics of each of the six Queens. This is further emphasized in the show by drawing on different pop tropes for each of the six, with each evoking a particular pop artist through their musical style. It is therefore a very clear example of music as dramaturgy where the character speaks their truth through musical characteristics.

London Road allows us to explore how we can use Laban efforts to look at a score at the micro-level. Because of the nature of the way that *London Road* was written, using verbatim techniques and allowing the music to mirror the exact inflections of the interviewees, the efforts work on a moment-to-moment basis. The nature of the spoken voice means that often it is the efforts that involve an indirect use of space that are most applicable. When we speak, the voice often naturally moves in an indirect pitch frequency fashion, and so it is this quality that has often been musicalized in the show. One such character in the show is the female who takes a taxi ride and sings 'A Bit of the Shudders', and who has this indirect quality to the pitch shape. Her vocal effort could be seen to be float – sustained, indirect and light – whereas the taxi driver she is talking to has a much less sustained quality. His vocal quality changes moment by moment between dab and flick depending on whether he has a direct or indirect pitch quality. His vocal quality is quick and light, and sometimes he will spend a few syllables on the same pitch (therefore direct and 'dab') before then having a short period of indirectness of pitch (therefore 'flick'). The indirectness of both of their vocal qualities is set against an instrumental contrast with a very direct, regular underscore: the directness of the xylophone in the orchestration gives a dab effort throughout, punctuating in a very regular manner allowing the rhythmic intricacy of the vocal line space. Also in the background, the sustained version of 'Silent Night' which comes in and out of the song provides a gliding effort, giving sustain to the backing of the song, where all other elements have a quick use of time. In *London Road* we see instances of vocal efforts changing moment to moment to reflect the inflection of the natural speech of the verbatim interviews, and we also see instances of layering different efforts between the instrumental backing and the vocals. Due to the nature of the technique method of composition for this show, the instrumental component to the song often acts as a bed over which the vocals can operate and the instrumental music and the vocal music often complement each other in their difference, bringing together a whole picture.

Summing up

Laban efforts can provide a shared language between dramatists of all forms on the musical. It has long been a framework for the consideration of character and acting work, as well as its original context of dance and movement. By extending this to a non-physical form in music, it widens the shared language and provides a means by which the composer can conceive of character in a physical sense and then 'translate' this into how that can be conveyed in music. We have seen that it is common to find a layering of efforts, so that different parts of the whole are portraying a different piece of the jigsaw puzzle. Efforts can be attributed on a larger scale at the level of a whole character's musical qualities throughout the show, and also on a smaller-scale level whereby the efforts can change depending on the moment-by-moment intentions of the character. We have seen that by changing one of the three categories that determines the effort, a character can portray variety but within the overall soundworld for themselves. For example, a character whose main effort might be dab (quick – direct – light), depending on their mood and circumstance they might most easily move to glide (by changing quick to sustained) or flick (by changing direct to indirect) or punch (by changing light to heavy). We now have tools for considering how we might approach the various musical elements and characteristics of our themes; now let's turn to looking at creating musical themes and spinning them throughout a musical.

4

Trunk themes and branch themes

We've discussed the world of themes, largely from a narratological perspective, and we have also looked at ways of conceptualizing character in such a way that it can aid musical translation. In this chapter we will focus more on tools for how all of this might play out in the creating process.

A note for the analyst

The discussion of trunk and branch themes below speaks directly to the composer of musical theatre as a suggested means for creating thematic development in a musical score. In the frequent absence of nuts-and-bolts techniques for how to compose for musical theatre on a detailed scale, this is an offering as a way that can create meaningful and coherent results. It does not, however, mean that in the canon of musical theatre, this is the method that composers have used. The idea that there are certain key themes in a musical, in both narratological and musical terms, is probably ubiquitous, and to this end, this conceptualization of trunk and branch themes may well be helpful to you as an analyst, but the specifics of these kinds of detailed compositional techniques may or may not be found in the musical that you are analysing. This is only to say please do not fret or struggle on to find them in any one show in particular if they are not there: focus on other elements of analysis we have discussed instead.

Trunk themes

How, in practice, can we work out what the main themes of the show might be? Steven Cohan and Linda Shires's work on the analysis of narrative fiction, *Telling Stories*, identifies that 'to analyse structure will seek to identify the most "stress-full" points of emphasis, pressure and strain organised by its structure' (Cohan and Shires 1998, p. 52). This is a helpful analogy to analyst and composer, and indeed the whole creative team. The most 'stress-full' points may be the place where themes are situated. 'Stress-full' does not necessarily mean anxiety induced, in the way that we might say something is 'stressful', but rather in the sense of what Chatman calls the 'kernels' of the narrative. The term 'kernel' finds its equivalent in other narratological works; for example, it equates to the 'noyau' of Barthes. Chatman explains Barthes's concept of the hermeneutic code whereby the noyau, or kernels, are the 'major events' which 'advance the plot by raising and satisfying questions … Kernels cannot be deleted without destroying the narrative logic' (Chatman 1980, p. 53). Satellites, on the other hand, enrich the story but are not essential to its progression: 'A minor plot event – a *satellite* – is not crucial in this sense. It can be deleted without disturbing the logic of the plot, though its omission will, of course impoverish the narrative aesthetically' (Chatman 1980, p. 54).

We have discussed how story and plot differ from each other, in that plot is the temporal ordering of the events that tells the story in the particular work in consideration. Claude Lévi-Strauss brings these two perspectives together to give simultaneous considerations of methods of syntagmatic analysis (that is regarding the surface structure of the ordering of events) and methods of paradigmatic analysis (i.e. the grouping of events into categories) and giving a more layered complexity to these viewpoints. Rather than the terminology of events, kernels and satellites, Lévi-Strauss highlights important elements of a myth as '*gross constituent units*' (Lévi-Strauss 1955, p. 431). His method involves identifying each of the most significant moments of a story and placing them in columns whereby you can read the sequence of events by reading horizontally, but vertically the events are grouped according to some kind of linking factor between them.

Lévi-Strauss acknowledges that to choose which moments of the story (also bear in mind that he was focusing on myths) are used in the analysis is a means of 'trial and error' (Lévi-Strauss 1955, p. 431) and that the analyst can only try out various solutions which seem to them to indicate that the whole myth is represented by these fragments of moments. The approach taken here to implement his method of grouping units of narrative into themes will differ from his original method in that three of the narratological guiding principles that have been explored will form the fundamental basis of determining the units, rather than matters of linguistics. These are: Chatman's concepts relating to kernels, the idea that units which produce changes of state are important, and third, Cohan and Shires's identification of stress-full points as helpful imagery. What this process results in is approximately four or five columns of events linked by some kind of theme and is usually a very revealing exercise in determining the primary themes of the show.

Let's try this process out on *Hadestown* to identify what the most significant or 'stress-full' parts of the show might be.

Hermes establishes the 'Road to Hell', making clear the two worlds of the show		
	Eurydice describes the state of eternal winter and famine	
		Orpheus and Eurydice meet and Orpheus asks her to marry him

		Orpheus is writing a song to make spring come again
Persephone arrives in the world with summertime, back from Hadestown		
Hades comes early to collect Persephone and take her back to Hadestown		
	Winter returns	
		Eurydice urges Orpheus to finish the song he is writing
Hades and Perspehone argue		
Hades goes to find someone who is grateful for the protection of Hadestown		
		Orpheus is distracted by desperately trying to finish the song
	Eurydice, desperate for food, follows Hades to Hadestown	

	Orpheus discovers Eurydice is gone and follows her to Hadestown	
	Orpheus tells Hades he is going to take Eurydice home	
Persephone persuades Hades to give them a chance of escape		
Hades confronts Orpheus and tells him to sing		
		Orpheus sings the final song – the story of Hades's and Persephone's love
Hades sets the conditions on which they can leave		
	Orpheus and Eurydice start walking	
	Orpheus is filled with doubt and looks behind and therefore breaks the agreement with Hades, meaning Eurydice must return to Hadestown	
		Persephone and Eurydice, with the company, honour Orpheus

This process of grouping units of narrative into like themes vertically, while charting the linear tale horizontally, reveals four key themes to the narrative of the musical, depicted by the four vertical columns. We might call the first column on the left 'Hades's Power', with all the units there related to Hades's desire for power and his possessiveness of all that is his kingdom. Alongside this is the story of his now-troubled marriage to Perspehone. The second column along speaks of the world's 'Desperation', and is particularly related to Eurydice's fortunes in the show, even though the understanding is that this state of harshness and famine is so for everyone in the world above ground. This column speaks to the one to its left – it is both because of Hades's quest for power and possessiveness that this state has occurred, and it is also because of this state of affairs that Eurydice follows Hades to Hadestown in desperation. The third column along is the love story of 'Orpheus and Euridyce'. Even though this turns out to be a story of tragedy, it is the strand of hope and optimism that runs through the musical. And finally, the fourth column represents Orpheus's gift portrayed through the song that he writes to return spring and prosperity to the world. This turns out to be a song of love, and it has the power to rekindle the beginnings of the relationship between Persephone and Hades. Despite its tragedy, the show ends with honouring Orpheus and his gift of love and hope in this way.

This technique reveals the handful of main themes in a musical based on the narrative. I call these the **trunk** themes, like the trunk of a tree; they are the main backbone thematically of the piece from a narrative or conceptual perspective. Using the kind of process that Lévi-Strauss outlines will reveal the narrative trunk themes, and it may be that in addition to this there are some character trunk themes. If you are opting for a leitmotif approach to your score, it may be of particular importance that there are one or two characters who need to have their own trunk theme too. Consider carefully whether your particular show is one where this is necessary, or whether the focus is on what the show *means*, played out by particular characters, or whether the crux of the piece centres around the characters themselves, as characters or personages. For example, a biographical musical about a certain person from history may well need the character's theme as its own trunk theme in addition to narrative trunk themes. In *Hadestown* the song that Orpheus is writing, in a sense, is a leitmotif for him as a character. However, its meaning is wider than that – he is writing it in order to bring prosperity back to the world, and in fact it transpires that the ones who benefit from the song are Hades and Persephone who hear the song of their former love together. There are other important character themes in *Hadestown* that are not revealed by Lévi-Strauss method above: primarily the workers in Hadestown and the three Fates. We can see that the workers form a chorus who represent the state of oppression in Hadestown. The Fates are an omnipresent guiding force, representative in mythology, as well as in the musical, of the path of one's life and its destiny. We have not spoken of Hermes, who plays such a key role in the musical. Because Hermes does not have his own story unfolding – he is the storyteller, the narrator – Hermes in a sense resides at a kind of meta level, alongside the audience. He is within the narrative and interacts with all the other characters – Orpheus is particularly close to him as his ward – but Hermes is omniscient in a way that the other characters are not. Hermes knows the end of the story. As such, his character is part of the means by which the show is related, as opposed to belonging to thematic material himself. His character's key song 'Road to Hell' returns throughout the musical, and is really important in that way, but it is a narrating device rather than a dramatic theme; in the first iteration of the song he introduces all the characters in a direct address storytelling style.

In my own composing process, each of the narrative trunk themes of the show has a musical trunk theme. In this way I usually end up with some key songs which are like 'master songs' – they are the musical trunk themes from which everything else stems. While this is not necessarily the way that others write musicals, we can see in *Hadestown* that there are some key songs in relation to the trunk themes. Taking the first trunk theme of Hades and his power, Hades's philosophy is conveyed through the song 'Why We Build the Wall', in which the workers respond to Hades's solo call lines in unison responses, as if they are indoctrinated by his viewpoints. The workers have their own choral theme throughout the musical which is indicative of the effect of Hades's oppression, expressed in 'Chant I', alongside the intermittent vocalized percussive effects which the workers contribute to the score throughout. The second theme of famine and eternal winter is largely synonymous with the theme of the Fates: the 'Ooo' line in 'Any Way the Wind Blows'. While we added both the Workers and the Fates to the main thematic material in consideration of character, not just narrative, in fact both of these groups of characters have thematic material bound up with other trunk themes: the workers with that of Hades and the Fates with the trunk theme of the eternal winter. The third trunk theme of Orpheus and Eurydice's love is established in 'Wedding Song'. However, their love story takes many twists and turns in the show, and there are a variety of songs that portray different aspects of their love. Rather, a link is made in 'Wedding Song' between their love and the fourth trunk theme: Orpheus's writing of the song. It is this fourth trunk theme that has the clearest musical theme, being the working out of the 'La' melody throughout the entire show. However, this melody is used and varied so much throughout the show that it comes to signify much more than the mechanics of Orpheus's writing the song. In 'Wedding Song' it is almost as if it is established as indicative of their love; certainly it is indicative of hope and love more widely throughout the musical, emanating from Orpheus. Orpheus and Eurydice's love story comes to be bound up with that between Hades and Persephone and this melodic theme, while it takes on connotations of their love, ultimately becomes the story of Persephone and Hades's love. A final consideration of trunk themes in *Hadestown* must refer back to the universal theme that we discussed in Chapter 2. There we discussed that the universal theme in the show is about love and trust and that can be seen reflected in the trunk themes: those regarding Hades and the state of poverty in the world are brought about by love and trust breaking down between Hades and Persephone, whereas the third and fourth trunk themes centre around the opposite, positive power of love and trust. However, ultimately it is a lack of trust, leading to doubt, that results in both Eurydice following Hades to Hadestown, and then finally in Orpheus looking behind him on the road out of Hadestown. We saw in Chapter 1 that the song 'When the Chips Are Down' encapsulates something important at the heart of the universal theme, asking the question about how we react when in times of desperation, and it is the Fates that carry this central thematic material. The collection of four trunk themes and the way they work in relation to the universal theme demonstrate the response to this question on either side of its negative and positive answers. Ultimately the Fates hold the material which is the balance point of that question, around which the two pairs of lovers and their various responses to the question operate.

Branch themes

Having identified the main handful of trunk themes let's examine the steps along the way that bring these narrative threads to fruition. I find there are often many sub-themes related to the main dramatic themes, and I call these **branch** themes, like branches that stem off from a tree trunk but are connected to the main stem. The music that goes with narrative branch themes then is musically related to its trunk theme.

When musical and visual material is first paired together, an association is made in the audience's mind such that that unit of music becomes infused with meaning. We have seen in Chapter 2 how this works semiotically in the language of signs. Once such a pairing is made, the music recalls the situation, event, character or emotion that it was placed with originally; any later use of the same music will carry that meaning with it. This is one of the most powerful tools in the arsenal of the composer as dramatist. Our job can be seen as infusing musical material with dramatic meaning, and then working with this meaning-infused music in order to tell stories. The traditional compositional methods of thematic development thereby take on added layers of significance when composing for musical theatre, because the forms that we are creating are governed by the storytelling, and it is this storytelling which is our primary purpose. Music must still make musical sense according to the syntax that governs music in a stand-alone capacity, but primarily we are ruled by the requirements of storytelling first. In that regard, the spinning of branch themes throughout a score to acquire, recreate or newly create meaning is of great significance to the process.

This can be achieved on a more or less conscious level in terms of noticeability for the audience. Reprise is perhaps the most noticeable version of recalling previous meaning musically: a section of music or a song is repeated, or reprised, later on in the piece to bring to mind the associations that music carries from earlier. Reprise is not in fact what I mean by a branch theme. It is, of course, an important tool in the musical and is a frequently found structural device, often involving an act two reprise of a song found in act one, or a way of book-ending a show with songs that open and close acts being in some form reprises of each other. A branch theme of the kind I am proposing is probably less noticeable to the audience but means that a score can be woven that sounds like it has a sense of coherent trajectory and means that thematic development of multiple musical strands is happening over the course of a musical.

Let us take an example trunk theme, such as 'jealousy'. Hypothetical branch themes might be used for moments that spark the jealousy, or for events arising out of it. It might be that there are subtopics related to the jealousy, such as an occurrence of manipulative behaviour, or one character winning over another: all of these moments in the musical might in some small way be musically related to the 'jealousy' theme but become their own song moments, and that is what I mean by branch themes. This is where the terminology of motifs and cells that we looked at in Chapter 2 comes into play. Musical themes might be broken down into smaller component units: motifs, or even smaller than that: cells.

And so, it is important for the musical theatre composer to decide why certain compositional techniques might be used in order to spin material. If we take the principle that everything we compose for musicals comes from dramaturgy, then the drama can help us decide how to spin branch themes.

Fragmentation

The first tool of spinning branch themes is fragmentation. This is the principle that the trunk theme can probably be split into much smaller fragments: cells. These might be two- or three-note cells providing the composer with specific, characteristic intervals which can be used in multiple ways. Fragmentation can be seen in 'Ex-Wives' from *Six* where the traditional melody of *Greensleeves* is broken up into cells of two or three notes to become stabs chords in the accompaniment. The melody is heard in its fragmented state as a harmonic foundation in the first verse of the song, before it is heard in its entirety as an instrumental section following the first chorus and then returning to its fragmented stop chord form for the following verse. One trunk theme might provide multiple cells, each one being then ripe for musical manipulation, some of the ways of which are explored below. It can be imagined that in this way an entire musical score can be derived from the trunk themes, without this involving lots of wholesale repetition (more than might be desirable in any case). Fragmented cells can also become starting points for thematic extension, whereby the initial fragment provides the beginning of a melody which then follows a new trajectory to its original tune. The embedding of fragments from the trunk theme into branch themes that are tangentially thematically related results in a score where the musical building blocks from one of the main dramatic themes in the show is interwoven throughout the score giving a strand of songs that feel like they are in some way offspring of the original parent theme. Even when there is no sharing of whole themes, or even motifs, between songs, this fragmentation and embedding approach results in a degree of cohesion which can be very unifying in the overall soundworld of a show. It is particularly useful in instances where multiple musical styles might be in use, or there might be multiple strands of storyline or interwoven relationships occurring in the narrative. Fragmenting and embedding enables the composer to think in relational strands, grouping together branch themes and relating them to a large-scale trunk theme in their mind. It helps not only the compositional process, but the resulting navigation of the score by the listener, even if on a subconscious level.

Repetition

Repetition is, of course, a much-used tool in composition of all kinds. From fugues, to symphonies, to punk rock, music seems to be based on sequences of establishing material and then repeating it in patterns of varying kinds. We've discussed reprise as one form of repetition, but I'd like to look at it on a smaller scale than that. The repetition of a motif might lead to a phrase. And then we might repeat those again in a second, repeated phrase. Take the beginning of 'A Part of That' from *The Last Five Years*: the melody of the verse here comprises a short cell which is repeated three times, followed by a fourth version which is a derivation of the cell. The three repeated cells and the final varied version are placed together to form a phrase. The second phrase begins as the first one did, and then this time it is the second part of the phrase that takes it elsewhere. Repetition helps to establish an idea. In this instance, dramatically, there is the repetition of a short cell that represents the normal, everyday patterns of life, and then it is when Cathy expresses that Jamie is off in his own world that the music changes into a more expansive melodic range, out of the repeated cell that has occurred to that point. Melodic repetition is used with significant effect in *London Road*. Due to the verbatim technique with which the show was created, song structures are formed from the specific repetition of certain units of the verbatim material. The repetition of these phrases creates structures akin to choruses, or repeated sections that root the score and the audience's ability to navigate it. For example, in songs like 'Everyone Is Very Very Nervous' and 'It Could Be Him' these title lines in the songs are the ones which are repeated – repetition here emphasizes the main point of that particular number, having selected that part of the verbatim phrase as the one which is going to act as a hook. This is a good example of spinning musical structures from material which, by its very nature, consisted of lots of independent motifs in its original state.

Repetition is also a harmonic device. You might know the repetition of motifs or cells by the terms 'ostinato', 'riff' or 'loop'. These terms indicate that it is a common occurrence in many genres of music, as they are usually used in the contexts of different styles. You might think of a riff as a four-bar guitar pattern that keeps repeating through a song. This would be a fairly standard thing to do, but if you are writing it with dramatic intention that might give us pause to question why we are doing it. This kind of repetition is a harmonic version compared with the melodic version seen above, and it could be interpreted dramatically as a means of being in one train of thought – like the musical equivalent of a paragraph. For example, in 'Get Down' in *Six* Cleves sings of all the many activities she is going to do in her capacity as a free woman, over a weighty bass riff which continues to loop until her change of thought which is directed straight at an imaginary Henry. At this change of harmonic sequence she sings of what happened between them that meant she ended up with this freedom. The third change of harmonic pattern is her declaration of complete independence, which brings about the return of the original harmonic pattern. While we can see that this also follows the song structural changes of a particular harmonic progression for verse, pre-chorus and chorus, these changes are also brought about by changes in thought and the specific focus of the lyrics at any one time.

This principle – that we might repeat in order to stay within one unit of a character's thought process or a unit of event happening dramatically, or to indicate something that is continually underlying what is happening in other layers of the drama – is one that we can apply to various situations and on various sizes of musical motif. We might have a very short ostinato – even as short as two notes – which continues to repeat while the rest of the musical language changes around it. This might dramatically suggest that something is 'stuck' without being able to move forward, or there is some kind of mental loop happening where a character is anxiously thinking around a certain issue, or it may infer business going on around the character or an impending sense of something about to happen.

It's important to think about the musical elements, and in which element the repetition is situated: for example whether there is a melodic loop or a harmonic riff or a bass-line ostinato. This is not to say that the music repeats itself wholesale – you can have a bass-line ostinato repeat through an entire song with the harmony and melodies continually shifting over the top (in classical music this is called a ground bass), or likewise a small two-note cell continuing incessantly to demonstrate the anxiety of a character while the other layers of music are shifting around it. As we explored in Chapter 3, our conceptualizing of a musical score in layers comes back in to play: in which layer of the music do you want the technique you are focusing on to be? Do other musical elements continue in a different way around it? Or does everything repeat in a very obvious loop, perhaps indicating in a much more obvious way a sense of being stuck in a certain place before moving onwards?

Augmentation and diminution

Augmentation elongates the note values of a cell or motif and as such is a rhythmic manipulation, usually by doubling them (a crotchet becomes a minim and so forth). In and of itself, it is likely to result in a change of 'effort' if such a manipulation were wanted for a particular theme, creating a version which is more laboured, paced or sustained; it changes the way that the motif operates within time. Note that it doesn't necessarily indicate a change in tempo overall – the musical context of the augmented line might be continuing at the same pace while that particular aspect doubles its time relatively. It can be a useful tool when wishing to subtly recall a theme within another context – the augmented motif can become a bassline or a middle harmony line, on top of which other melodic material occurs. When wishing to fuse two sung themes together in a more evident fashion, augmenting one of them can result in being able to distinguish one vocal theme from the other a little more clearly.

The opposite of augmentation is diminution whereby a cell or motif's note values are shortened, usually by half. A motif in diminution might stand alone, or might become a loop, as discussed above, within a different musical context, with other material going on around it.

Melody becomes harmony

It can be seen that amongst the suggested uses of augmentation and diminution above, some techniques involve taking melodic material and making it harmonic material: this is seen in the case of the ground bass technique, which implies harmonic language, or in the motif in diminution that becomes a riff, again implying a harmonic sequence. There are further extensions of the melody-becomes-harmony technique that can be used to embed thematic material within new musical contexts. One such is to turn melodic material into chords. We have discussed horizontal versus vertical elements of music, and this is a way in which horizontal can become vertical by taking a few pitches that occur next to each other in a melody, and grouping them together in a chord, and then taking a few more pitches from another fragment of the melody and making them another chord, and so on. Very often this might result in cluster chords, and it is not a technique that works for all melodies. However, when the fragments are carefully chosen, it is a useful tool to be able to encode thematic material as a branch theme into a new musical context, when you might be wanting to subtly recall a particular theme.

Retrograde

Melodic retrograde is a technique which involves turning a motif or cell around the other way, starting at the end and playing the sequence from the end to the beginning. It can be used to subtly recall melodic themes without an obvious sense of recognition, or used as a metaphor for a particular dramatic theme or character finding a change in their circumstances, a literal turning upside down of life events or turning the issue on its head. This melodic manipulation would be a very literal parallel to such a dramatic event.

Harmony and tonality

The tools so far have mostly involved horizontal elements of music being manipulated but fragmenting the harmony of trunk themes can also be a useful tool. The principle of retrograde can be related to harmony whereby a section of harmonic sequence in a trunk theme can be turned round and played the other way to create new harmonic patterns and creating the harmonic foundation for new melodies. There is much that can be done to create strands of songs that feel subtly cohesive in relation to the trunk theme via tonal relations, for example, using closely related keys. The closely related keys to a tonic key (I) are those built on the subdominant (IV) and dominant (V), plus the relative major or minor to each of those—so six closely related keys in total. Sharing fragments of harmonic language between branch songs also creates a kind of unity that very subtly bind these songs to the trunk theme master song. In reality, I completely acknowledge that changing keys to suit performers' ranges is common practice within the world of musical theatre; however, this kind of tonal relationship can be an ideal to strive for, if vocal ranges are then carefully considered within each song.

Let's look at the example of *Hadestown,* where the song that Orpheus is writing acts as a leitmotif throughout the show, as we have already identified. The motifs of the song are musically manipulated, recontextualized and varied throughout the show and provide a good example of the spinning of thematic material. Orpheus's song material is first encountered in the opening number 'Road to Hell' when Hermes introduces Orpheus, along with the rest of the characters. Orpheus sings his melody as the first introduction to himself as a character, establishing the distinctive contours of the phrases, or motifs, of the melody. It is fragmented here, sung in response to Hermes's line. We only hear the first two motifs of the melody, and even then the second phrase is slightly curtailed from its later versions. 'Road to Hell' is in a 4/4 time signature and so the version of the melody that we hear at this point is in 4/4, in the context of the root song 'Road to Hell'. However, the melody in its fundamental version is not in 4/4. How do we know this? Given that this is the first statement of it, would it not make sense that this is the foundational, original version of the melody? The answer to this is a dramatic one. Because Orpheus is writing the song throughout the show, and says repeatedly to Eurydice that it is not yet finished, the final version of the song is therefore the root version of it. It is the final version of the song in 'Epic III' where we hear Orpheus's melody in its entirety. It is here in the context of the story that Orpheus has finished his song, and so we take to mean that all previous versions of the melody are in the context of Orpheus working it out, within multiple other song scenarios. In the final version, the wordless melody, sung to 'la' is in 6/4 and has a triple metre feeling of lilt to it.

The second time the melody is heard is in 'Wedding Song' when Eurydice asks to hear the song so far, and Orpheus sings four phrases for her. This iteration is in 4/4, as was the case in 'Road to Hell', but this time the second motif that was heard in 'Road to Hell' which is left suspended and unfinished, becomes the fourth phrase with motifs 2 and 3 being heard in between the opening and closing motifs.

It is in 'Epic I', when Hermes reminds Orpheus of the tale of the gods that he heard long ago, that the melody takes on it 6/4 format, as if this sparking of Orpheus's memory of the tale sets the melody into its rightful time signature and feel. In this iteration, phrases 1 and 4 maintain the shape that they had previously, but phrase 2 adopts its characteristic fall to the major 3rd, in contrast with the resolution to the minor chord of phrases 1 and 3. Phrase 4 maintains its suspension and sense of being unfinished. This is in fact the full version of the melody which is found in 'Epic III', and so is in a dramatic sense the finished 'la' chorus. In 'Epic I' the chorus melody is paired for the first time with a recitative-like storytelling section before it, as Orpheus recounts the tale of the gods that Hermes has told him. This develops throughout 'Epic II', and into 'Epic III' where it is through this recitative that Orpheus recites Hades's story and what has become of him back to him. This is the part of the song that has unfolded in the show to this point: the chorus itself is recalled by Orpheus and therefore in some way 'finished' early on in the show, but it is the storytelling part of the song that goes with it that he has had to learn through experience in the narrative, and therefore that is the part that is finally finished in 'Epic III'. The completion of this melody in its 'finished' form in a sense is the musical resolution of Orpheus's journey, but this is in fact not the case – he has finished the song, but it is a false ending. Throughout the show, the song has been imbued with several associations and has become a semiotic sign for several things: Orpheus's special gifts in 'Road to Hell'; a promise of hope for spring to come again and the seasons to right themselves in 'Wedding Song'. Both of these are in their 4/4 version, and in that iteration, they are more aligned with the narrative of Orpheus and Eurydice, their love story and their holding on to hope, as previously discussed. In the various versions of 'Epic', the melody is associated increasingly with Hades and Persephone, and with their love story that has gone wrong, and hence thrown the seasons out of kilter. In the 6/4 version, the sign is more strongly one of the two gods and their story. 'Epic III' is not, however, the end of the story of this song, as it is heard again in 'Doubt Comes In' in fragmentation. Orpheus and Eurydice are making their perilous journey back out of hell, forbidden from looking at each other. As doubt rages in Orpheus's head, there are a couple of interludes in which he sings motifs from the melody, this time back to its 4/4 version and in fragmented motifs, as was heard at the beginning of the show. This feels symbolic of Orpheus trying to hold on to the hope that was created through the song, in the version of it that is representative of his own love story. Its fragmentation, however, implies a breaking down of his ability to hold on to this; and musically this is foreshadowing what indeed turns out to be the case.

Summing up

The possibilities of thematic spinning are as endless as your imagination. The point I hope to make is that a score can have a very intricate web of patterns and relationships between songs that align with dramatic relationships in multiple ways. The dramaturgy and the score can work in an entirely integrated way together; the composer is as much a part of the dramaturgy in the musical through this interrelation approach to the score. The collaboration between members of the creative team is therefore crucial; the composer's view of the themes in the piece needs to be born out of all of the conversations going on between writer, director and designer regarding the themes that are being brought out in all other aspects of the musical. It has been said before that I am thematically obsessed, and I think that is probably the case! But thematic composition is such a friend to the composer for so many reasons. It helps the flow of collaborative practice between drama and music; it keeps us constantly asking 'why' when we are making musical choices while composing; it provides the foundation for creating a palette of building blocks from which to populate an entire score; and it results in something that can sound cohesive no matter how far the particular musical is wanting to stretch in terms of wide-ranging style. For me, themes are the essence of composing for musicals. What we will look at next is how we create shapes from the pallette.

The second shared language: Shape

Section Two will focus on exploration of the language of **shape**. This section is also divided into four chapters, each exploring what **shape** might mean in relation to musical theatre. Chapter 5 will look at the concept of the dynamic curve, and how sketching two-dimensional shapes can help to visualize the temporal and three-dimensional shape of a musical. Chapter 6 looks at modes of enunciation, how they differ from performance modes and how consideration of these combined can help to create or release intensification. Chapter 7 will look at big, structural shapes in the musical, looking at the dynamic curve in practice, while Chapter 8 looks at small shapes and the smaller-scale level of song structuring and the shaping of musical phrases.

The musicals which will be drawn on for study in Section Two are:

- *35MM: A Musical Exhibition*
  Music and Lyrics by Ryan Scott Oliver
  Based on photographs by Matthew Murphy

- *Come From Away*
  Book, Music and Lyrics by Irene Sankoff and David Hein

- *Dear Evan Hansen*
  Book by Steven Levenson
  Words and Music by Benj Pasek and Justin Paul

- *In the Heights*
  Music and Lyrics by Lin-Manuel Miranda
  Book by Quiara Alegría Hudes
  Conceived by Lin-Manuel Miranda

- *Matilda the Musical*
  Book by Dennis Kelly
  Music and Lyrics by Tim Minchin
  Author Roald Dahl

- *Sue Townsend's The Secret Diary of Adrian Mole Aged 13³/₄ The Musical*
  Book and Lyrics by Jake Brunger
  Music and Lyrics by Pippa Cleary

- *The Light in the Piazza*
  Book by Craig Lucas
  Music and Lyrics by Adam Guettel

5

Dynamic curves

Shape is a powerful collaborative tool: it applies to the structure of the whole musical; to a character's dramatic arc; to the journey of a song; to a consideration of the balance of score versus dialogue; the list goes on. Considerations of shape apply to every member of the creative team, be it through the visual shapes of a designer, or the more conceptual shapes of story arc or melodic phrasing.

Shape: Some definitions

The word 'shape' can function as a noun, meaning the form of something given by its outer edge or contours. This might be a geometric shape, such as a triangle, a square or a circle. Or it might be a more nebulous form such as might be conceived while making out some kind of shape from a cloud formation. We also use the term to indicate the relative health of something, be it physical health – 'that person is in good shape' – or to refer to the financial health of an organization, or the qualities of a choir's performance for example: these too might be said to be in 'good shape'. The word can also be a verb, whereby a potter shapes their clay – in this instance shaping a physical object – or where a person might shape their response to another, and therefore not shaping anything tangible in the physical sense.

In the case of creating musical theatre, it can be seen that several of these meanings can be drawn on when we use the term 'shape'. All of the collaborators involved in the process of creating the musical in some way shape it, in the verbal

     The Musical Theatre Composer as Dramatist

sense of the word; a fact which speaks again of the crucial nature of collaboration in the creation of musical theatre. The primary use of the word going forward will relate to the contours that might be conceptualized by the musical, and thereby thinking of it as a noun: the 'shape' created by the show playing out through time. This is a conceptual idea whereby we think of something that is experienced through time as being able to be represented by way of a line drawing that demonstrates an idea of the shape it is creating. The crucial factor that we will be exploring that creates this shape is the idea of 'intensification'; in other words how heightened or otherwise the drama is at any one moment in time. How high are the stakes? How intense is the emotion? How much does the music have you by the emotional throat? How much intensity is created through all of the performance elements happening at the same time, creating an overwhelming sense of audiovisual sensory stimulus? If this kind of idea of shaping were to be thought of as being presented graphically on a pair of axes, the horizontal axis would represent 'time' – the unfolding of the show as a temporal medium – and the vertical axis would represent 'intensification' – how intense it is (brought about by various factors) at that moment in time.

The dynamic curve

The resulting shape can be referred to as the 'dynamic curve'; the term that musicologist Kofi Agawu uses when exploring the idea in relation to classical leider (song). Agawu's basic dynamic curve, used to represent a kind of 'standard' of the typical shaping of a classical song, ascends to a highpoint and then descends again, as demonstrated by the reproduction of Agawu's basic curve shape below.

Agawu's dynamic curve

(Agawu 1984, p. 162)

The dynamic curve has a plethora of uses when creating, or analysing, musical theatre. The basic curve shape shown here gives us a starting point: it indicates that the unit being considered (be that the shape of the whole show, or the shape of a song for example) might have a period of growth, reach a moment of climax and then lower in intensity again to some kind of stability – although notably not falling to the original starting level. While this might be recognizable as a classic narrative shape, common to many art forms be they story, music or dance, this is however merely a starting point. When used as a tool for creation, the dynamic curve can enable you to conceptualize whatever shape is appropriate for the particular work you are creating. It can be used, for example, to consider the desired shape of the narrative alone, the score alone, a particular scene or an individual song. It is perhaps at its most valuable when it enables consideration of the shape of all of the elements of the musical in their collaboration. This is a framework which is often lacking as an analytical or writing tool. As we have already said many times, musicals are created by multiple people, disciplines and art forms all working together, and being able to find a common language to articulate how those disciplines are all working together and what kind of shape they are creating in their totality is valuable. It can be used as a problem-solving tool, when a moment doesn't seem to be working or a particular section of a show seems to lack drive. We are moving forward with the exploration of the dynamic curve on the basis that musicals – and the drama found in musicals, as with any kind of storytelling – are constructed through the shaping of periods of heightening tension and releasing it again, and that this process happens many times within the course of a whole musical on various levels of scale. Large-scale shapes might build to one main peak of intensification over the course of the whole show, but once you drill down to the smallest-scale level of the musical phrase shape, the process of heightening and releasing can be seen to be happening on multiple levels all at the same time throughout the whole show. We are assuming that a flat line (at whatever level of intensification) as a dynamic curve shape would not constitute drama if sustained for too long a time period. Using the concept of the dynamic curve to get inside what is happening in terms of the shapes being created can help to pinpoint why a section might be falling flat, or how the shape of the show might be changed by a move in positioning of a song for example. In the instance of working on a musical adaptation of a pre-existing story, the dynamic curve of the original can be worked out and then considered as part of the collaborative discussions for how to go about adapting the work. It's worth noting that the musicalization of anything will change the dynamic curve's contours.

Intensification

The dynamic curve is a tool for interpretation, rather than an exact science. The notion of intensity (the vertical axis) is difficult to measure and thus complex in terms of representing it graphically in this way. No absolute measurement can be given to an axis of intensity, and therefore the parameters must be defined by each individual analyst or creative, and considered in relative terms within the scale of the axis. The intensity being represented in the diagram could be considered either as emotional intensity, or as structural intensity, or, most likely, both of these.

Emotional intensity

There is a traditional saying in musical theatre that when speaking is no longer enough to express a character's thoughts they sing, and when singing doesn't suffice, they dance. Such a view really belongs to the more traditional forms of 'book' musical such as the integrated musical and the megamusical. In musicals that are driven by narrative, the notion of the 'integrated musical' is one which is commonly referred to, suggesting the manner in which the multiple performance modes of a musical are unified by their function of serving the plot. Integration has been a key concept in musical theatre since the work of Rodgers and Hammerstein in the so-called Golden Age of musical theatre between the 1940s and 1960s. Rather than favouring the song and dance element of the musical as the early musical comedy had done, Rodgers and Hammerstein have been commonly attributed with the idea of making the plot the key feature. Integration implies that the performance modes of song, dance and dialogue serve the plot and the conveyance of story and character. To this end, Hammerstein wrote dialogue and lyrics in the vernacular of each specific character to ensure a more believable sense of tone to the words of the musical. The model of the integrated musical suggests a prominent level of collaboration in the creative process, whereby each element of the show is created to add meaning to the story conveyed by the whole. *Oklahoma!* is often considered as the first integrated musical (although *Show Boat* stood as pioneering in this regard two decades previously) and the canon of Rodgers and Hammerstein thought fundamental in the instigation of this way of writing. However, for several of the musicals we are exploring, integration would not be the appropriate descriptor. Indeed, the boundaries that define musical theatre in the contemporary age are ever-evolving such that we often move away from the book musical entirely. However, there are perhaps a few key features of the integrated musical which remain, even in more experimental versions of the musico-dramatic form and which lead us to this fundamental question: in the broadest sense possible, does a song usually occur at a key moment of emotional energy?

Since the rise of the megamusical in the 1980s, the raising of emotional intensity in the musical has taken an even more significant turn. The term 'megamusical' was developed in the field by Jessica Sternfeld in *The Megamusical* (2006) and has since been used to denote a large-scale musical with epic proportions and with the dominance of spectacle. One of the features of the megamusical genre is the use of each performance language to bring about theatrical heightening with a view to instigating a high level of emotional affect. Vagelis Siropoulos (2010) has discussed the overwhelming effects brought about by musicals of the subgenre through the use of emotional intensification in his article. In '*Evita*, the Society of the Spectacle and the Advent of the Megamusical' Siropoulos furthers his ideas about the megamusical as a platform for engulfing the audience in a sensory experience:

> To put it simply, the megamusical aspires to be a feast for both the eyes and ears. The audience is not so much invited to identify emotionally with characters or think; they are primarily invited to hear and see: to re-educate their liberated sense and learn to indulge in purely aural and optical

situations; to feel the sound in their guts and be absorbed by the visuals. Thus, the spectators cease to be onlookers, observers of the action and are swallowed up in it, devoured by the spectacle itself.

(Siropoulos 2010, p. 171)

There is a physical response which is brought into play in which the introduction of song creates a change in sensory perception which brings about a sense of heightened trajectory. Due to the excessive proportions of the megamusical, as Siropoulos notes, the levels of audiovisual stimulation may bring about a perception of sensory overwhelm, provoking a sense of heightened response at particular moments in the musical's trajectory. While the element of spectacle is a defining feature of the megamusical, and the musicals that have been developed in the genre's legacy, the idea of spectacle and heightening of emotional affect has always been of significant importance to the musical. The Broadway conductor Lehman Engel's thoughts on the definition of the musical, originally written in 1972, are interesting on this. His key characteristics of the genre, set out in *Words with Music: Creating the Broadway Libretto*, are: 'Feeling – Romance – Lyrics and Particularisation – Comedy – Subplot – Music' (Engel 2006, p. 73). Of these characteristics, he believes *feeling* to be of primary importance, rather than any one particular performance mode. His definition of *feeling* implies not just an outpouring of emotion but one which results in empathetic characterization, and a truth at the heart of the work, however fantastical its setting. It implies that it is the journey of character that lies at the heart of a piece of musical theatre's success. The idea of inciting emotion and having the intention to 'affect' is one that will be explored further in the next chapter on modes of enunciation.

Engel's view supports an argument that no single element of the musical is of primary importance, and in fact storytelling, or the exploration of an idea, is the root of everything that follows. Engel's original publication date of 1972 places his thoughts in a particular era; for example, this was before the emergence of the megamusical movement. It was also before the full exploration of the plot-less concept musical; a form of musical theatre in which there is no linear narrative of causation but rather the central component of the show is a single idea or concept. The importance Engel places on subplot cannot be said to be particularly relevant in relation to the concept musical. However, Engel's fundamental idea that *feeling* is key relates to the ideas of the emotional intensity hypothesis and of sensory overwhelm already discussed, and it is interesting to note further where *feeling* might be located in the musical. While Engel places it with character and plot, in *The Broadway Musical: A Critical and Musical Survey* Joseph Swain highlights the potential importance of music as regards the portrayal of feeling:

> Whether music in the theatre can really be an essential dramatic force has been a matter of some contention. If drama is a product of words alone, then any musical adaptation must weaken the drama, because music is in general abstract, without explicit semantic reference … When the important actions are actions of feeling, or emotion, then music not only suffices, it surpasses the power of words to define the action … The broad semantic range typical of western music, the very quality that makes it unsuitable for conveying fact and idea, makes it an ideal symbol of psychological or emotional action.
>
> (Swain 2002, p. 1)

These ideas regarding emotion and *feeling* are of clear importance to the genre of musical theatre, but the way in which they are evoked in the musical is harder to quantify. This category of *feeling* can be seen as related to our scale of intensification and therefore be used as a parameter to create the dynamic curve, thereby providing a visual shape as a representation of how elements of *feeling* are evoked through the structuring of the work.

Structural intensity

Independently of the emotional intensity, or perhaps rather in combination with it, the intensification on the vertical axis of the dynamic curve might be conceptualized as related to the particular performance mode or discipline being used at any one time, or of other structural elements of the musical. The question might be: how are the various performance disciplines sitting together and interrelating in order to create the desired shape?

We have discussed the integrated musical, but Scott McMillin, in *The Musical as Drama*, challenges the notion of integration (even in musicals from the heyday of the so-called integrated musical) because of the implication that performance elements *seamlessly* integrate, as if they become one and the same mode of expression. Dominic Symonds has also highlighted in his work (2005) the fact that speech and song are in fact perceived as *different* from each other, thus suggesting a flaw in the concept of the seamless, integrated whole of the musical. McMillin also puts forward the argument that it is in fact the very difference between the component performance elements of the musical that is used to such effect, rather than an imagined fusing of these disparate modes of performance into one. Not only does each mode involve a different manifestation of performance, but speech, song and dance can be seen to play out a different perspective of time from each other. Speech more generally portrays a sense of 'real' time unfolding whereas song and dance can change the audience's temporal perception and either prolong or contract periods of time. McMillin's ideas regarding difference do not simply relate to the literal, physical differences between speech, song and dance, but propose that on entering each of these performance modes there is a shift in temporal perception. He calls these 'two orders of time, one for the book and one for the numbers' (McMillin 2006, p.6). McMillin calls the first order of time 'book time' and the second order of time 'lyric time'. His view is that musicals are not truly integrated, but that the two timeframes co-exist side by side in *coherence.*

We have already posed the question about whether songs happen at moments of intensity; however, it is also appropriate to consider this question in reverse and to explore whether moments of song, or number, *create* emotional intensity in themselves, through being heightened forms of presentation. It is implicit in McMillin's ideas that there is a change in dramatic dynamic when transferring from speech into song. Such a shift and change in dramatic dynamic in itself creates an intensification of emotion, from a naturalistic mode of presentation (speech) to a heightened form (song or dance). Rather than simply considering the change from speech into song, each aspect of performance in the musical can be seen to have a more naturalistic form, and a more heightened form: dialogue or spoken prose transforms into metrical lyrics; naturalistic character movement or physical interaction becomes dance or stylized movement; the visual creation of a particular world, time or place can be transformed into a more technical spectacle. Within the consideration of music as a heightened form in itself, difference in intensity can be identified between the use of underscoring as potentially less intense than the foregrounding of music that occurs within song. These performance elements combine in a variety of configurations: for example, lyrics combine with music to form song; combined song and dance; or the combination of song with technical spectacle.

The following diagram portrays these ideas of intensification. Musical theatre is a complex web of interwoven storytelling techniques, which exist on differing levels of intensity, as is seen by the diagram's multiple levels.

Intensification chart

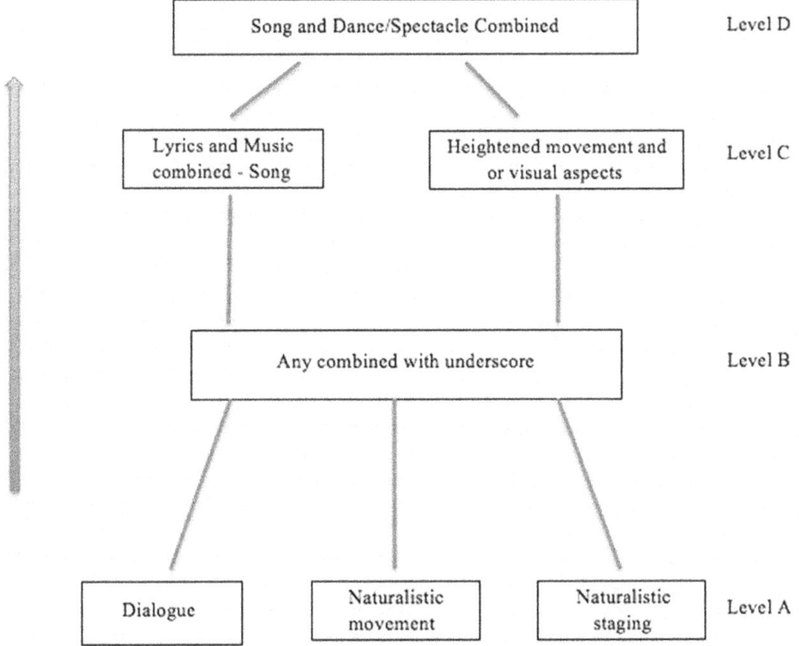

Level A is representative of a more naturalistic style of theatre, comprising dialogue between characters in scenes, with relatively naturalistic movement, potentially with underscored music at level B. Each of these aspects is heightened: dialogue becomes regulated and more poetic in the form of lyrics; music comes to the forefront taking on more formal structures. Naturalistic movement is heightened to provide dance in a similar process to speech becoming lyrics. It can be seen in each of these examples that the heightening takes on an increased level of formalization. An intensification of performance mode also brings about a more formalized mode of presentation. The visual aspects of musical theatre have become increasingly important in the post-megamusical era of the current Broadway and West End stage. Visual staging therefore also has a level of heightening to level C in the form of technical spectacle. Level D demonstrates combinations of the individual heightened forms seen at level C. The greater the number of heightened modes which are combined, the greater the levels of perceptual stimulation and therefore the greater the intensification of affect. Within the modes of storytelling of level C there exist a number of combinations and planes on which meaning is being portrayed: the lyrics/music plane to provide song; the dance/music plane; the lyrics/music/dance trifold plane to provide the song and dance number. The different combinations of heightened performance elements themselves therefore also present a scale of intensification, according to the number being combined at any moment. The point at level D represents the four-way plane at which point all elements are combined: lyrics/music/dance/technical or visual spectacle. The arrow on the left of the diagram represents the sliding scale of perceptual intensity, increasing up the levels of heightened states. It is the *combination* of level A with levels B, C and D which may be considered a particular defining characteristic of the musical theatre as a genre. The musical moves between the levels of intensification, in different combinations of performance elements.

However, the levels of intensity of *performance mode* (speech, song, dance) do not necessarily equate to a level of intensity of the *emotional* response perceived. It is important that these factors are separated, especially in consideration of the fact that emotional response is by no means a uniform factor. Similarly, we do not want to carry forward a sense of 'intensity' necessarily referring to the concept of size (e.g. loudness of dynamic, numbers of cast). This is one means by which sensory heightening can occur, but, as we shall see later in the book, sometimes it is brought about by the opposite of largess; by a stripping back to bareness. The intensification diagram here acts as a visual example of how layers of heightening of performance modes are an important consideration in charting the course of intensification, but particularly in the case of more contemporary musicals, how these building blocks are then played with is often more experimental and creative than any diagram can represent.

Let's have a look at how some of our case study musicals use the interplay of performance modes as a shaping tool.

Matilda has a relatively traditional, integrated approach to performance elements: the show is a book musical in structure which has substantial scenes in which sit musical numbers. Choreography is used to heighten, involving large company numbers with choreography playing a significant part. *Adrian Mole* is similar in its approach. The levels of the intensification chart above can be seen to be directly relatable to these two shows, where both pieces traverse up and down across all levels, increasing and releasing heightened performance modes, and combining performance modes together to create rich accumulations of heightened intensification. The score in this regard functions as being in the form of numbers which the scene arrives at, navigating the transition between scene and song at the appropriate point. For both *Matilda* and *Adrian Mole,* the score could be viewed on the levels of intensification from the perspective of the structural placement of numbers within the musical, as well as how those numbers are relating to the stress-full points of the narrative and relating to the intensification of narrative stakes and emotions. *Dear Evan Hansen* also places songs within book scenes, but with less of an emphasis on dance than the previous two musicals. As we shall see later in this section, the songs often function as emotional indicators in this musical, and so to relate the intensification scale to indicators of *feeling* assists in understanding an important function of the music in the show.

In very different ways from each other, *In the Heights* and *Come From Away* share a technique of using spoken voice with sung voice in the numbers of their respective shows. *In the Heights* has an additional stage of formalized heightening of vocals through the use of rap: the voice is still at the timbre of spoken word but the rhythmic, formalized nature of the lyrics through rap heightens beyond naturalistic speaking. *In the Heights* fuses together rap with sung material, often creating shaping within numbers through moving continuously between the two. In *Come From Away*, there are few numbers that do not have spoken dialogue woven within them. It is one of the characteristics of the show that numbers often become extended musical sequences where underscored dialogue happens within the course of the song. This enhances both the direct storytelling and the communal shared experience which are important aesthetics with the show. For both of these shows, the structural shaping as regards performance modes is intricate *within* the songs, not just regarding the interface between the scene and song and the placing of song within that. Those considerations do not stop at the entry to song in these two musicals, but rather the continual charting of spoken word and sung lyrics continues throughout the score as well.

This is also the case in *The Light in the Piazza* whose songs do not necessarily adhere to familiar structuring devices. There are spoken scenes in the show, making it essentially a book musical, and yet large regions of the show are sung, and as we shall see, sometimes through-composed, thereby making much of the piece at a heightened level of performance mode intensification. The relative proportion of one particular performance mode in a show by definition alters how ideas of intensification via performance modes operates. *35MM* is entirely sung, and, crucially, is more akin to a song cycle: it is not a book musical with a linear narrative. The intensification chart as presented on p. 83 would not apply in that way to *35MM* because the show is not moving between registers of performance mode: this remains the same throughout. The show is entirely sung and consists of sequential numbers, each one standing alone, inspired by one of the collection of Matthew Murphey's photographs. The strap line of the show as a 'musical exhibition' portrays that the show is structurally like experiencing a collection – the moments are somehow thematically related to each other within an umbrella, and connections between them can be brought out. But essentially they are also a series of moments to be taken as individual vignettes and appreciated in that way. It is human nature that when items are placed together we try to find the connections between them and so this seems inevitable that connections between the songs and the characters in each of the songs will be experienced, but the show does not function in the way that the book musical does by placing particular performance modes at particular moments in order to create a particular shape and heightening at that point in the narrative. Instead, as we shall see later in this section, the concept of intensification and changing degrees of intensity experienced over time is still completely relevant to a show such as *35MM*; however, the way this is conceived of differs from a musical with a linear narrative. In this instance the building and releasing of intensification have to be thought of by using different parameters than the changing of performance modes.

Summing up

In this chapter we have encountered the idea of the dynamic curve as a means of conceptualizing shape in musicals. We have defined this shaping as being related, by some and varying parameters, to the concept of intensification, and that the musical is a genre which rides the waves of intensification, building and heightening intensity over time and then releasing it, in order to build it up again, and release it again. This build and this release are primary building blocks of musicals. As with each of the tools we are looking at, the basic tool can be used in many different ways and remains applicable across all sub-genres of musico-dramatic works. Some of the more traditional ways of using intensification, such as that which is often referred to as 'song spotting' – deciding where in the narrative the songs are going to sit – are just one way of thinking of intensification. In other, and more experimental, forms of the genre, the concept of riding the waves of intensification is just as important, but needs to be thought of in different ways. Which parameters are placed under the magnifying glass in order to put the tool into practice is at the discretion of the creator or analyst. We have made a start by thinking about performance modes as one of those parameters, and in the next chapter we will use a different parameter which will change the nature of how that vertical axis of our dynamic curves – that which is measuring intensity – is viewed.

6

Modes of enunciation

In the previous chapter we looked at performance modes in terms of literal modes of expression: a character speaks, a character sings, a character dances. However, there is another way of thinking about this in terms of the function of any one moment in the musical, and that is through what Kofi Agawu calls 'modes of enunciation': 'enunciation' in the sense of pronouncing or expression. So far we have considered very literally whether it is appropriate for someone to speak, sing or dance in any one moment, and this concept takes that a step further in terms of how shape might be expressed. We looked at speaking relating to what McMillin calls 'book time' and singing to the term 'lyric time', but rather than expressing changes of performance mode in relation to types of 'time', Agawu's concept regarding 'modes of enunciation' can be used to determine the ways in which the significance of the changes of performance mode might be more conceptual. This is for the purpose of helping make a judgment regarding the level of intensification created. Rather than considering speech, song and dance modes as literal performance expressions, Agawu defines them conceptually in such a way that the 'mode' may be applied to any of the literal performance media. His definitions of the modes of enunciation focus on the intention of portrayal, or the mode's purpose. Speech mode has a '"telling" characteristic' (Agawu 2009, p.99), from which song and dance mode both depart. Song mode has a purpose to 'affect', and dance mode has a sense of bringing about energetic drive. Agawu describes the move from speech mode to song mode, and then dance mode in this way: 'The impulse to inform or deliver a conceptually recoverable message is overtaken by an impulse to affect, to elicit a smile brought on by a beautiful turn of phrase … While the dance mode often includes song, its most marked feature is a sharply profiled rhythmic and metric sense' (Agawu 2009, p. 99).

Within these definitions there are many possibilities for each literal performance mode to take on different modes of enunciation. For example, the fact that a song occurs does not necessarily imply that the song mode of enunciation has been reached. Similarly, it would be possible for a poetic, emotionally charged piece of dialogue or soliloquy to take on the enunciation mode of song, even though literally it is still in the performance mode of speech. If the purpose of song mode, according to Agawu, is to 'affect', then it is perhaps likely that a release of emotional tension may occur in song mode, but this may not necessarily be when a literal song occurs. Similarly, a moment of accumulated tension may correlate with the increased rhythmic impetus of dance mode, although this may not necessarily occur through dance. Let's break down each of these modes of enunciation and look at some examples in practice. I will continue to refer to literal forms of speech, song and dance using the term 'performance modes', whereas discussion of the conceptual speech, song and dance mode will be referred to as 'modes of enunciation'. Because our focus is on the score of the musical, we will be looking at examples of the different modes of enunciation occurring in the performance mode of song. However, any performance mode could assume the role of any of the three modes of enunciation.

The 'speech' mode of enunciation

Agawu defines speech mode as having a 'telling characteristic'. So when might that be useful? In terms of intensification, I propose that speech mode has the lowest intensity. It is for the conveyance of information, for a conversation between characters, for exposition; material that helps move plot forward in a relatively low-key way. This probably immediately sounds like a job for the book writer in our minds, but as we have said, the modes of enunciation cross over the boundaries of performance modes and it is highly likely that a composer will have to write some material in speech mode. But if we tend to go along the line of argument, as discussed in Chapter 5, that in a musical a character sings whenever the emotion is heightened, why would we ever sing the kind of material that speech mode implies? The answer to this in part winds back to the discussion in Chapter 1 on the essence of the show, the essence of the score and what your relative proportion of each performance mode is in the context of the show as a whole. It has for centuries been the case that in opera there is a form of singing which has a 'telling characteristic': it's called recitative. Because in opera the entire musico-dramatic form is through-sung, the lower intensity conveyance of information has to also be sung. The world of opera therefore developed a form of singing whereby the words were prioritized with the musical content taking a backseat: melodies are less expansive, rhythmic patterns are more natural and in line with natural speech patterns, harmony tends to be sustained or punctuated in order to allow the vocal line to convey its message. We see this same idea in musical theatre. We find in the innovative style of Lin-Manuel Miranda, that the combination of rap and sung material in *In the Heights* (and in *Hamilton*) plays on this same idea of using a genre of music that enables a lot of words to be expressed and prioritizes the lyrics in the rap sections, while using fewer words and more expressive musical material in the sung sections. If there is a lot of music in your show, then there need to be ways of lowering and heightening the intensity of that music: it can't all be highly expressive or the ear tires of the relentless intensity and emotion.

'Benny's Dispatch' is an example of a song in *In the Heights* which is in speech mode, but not because the vocal line is not pitched. The song begins with simply a bass line over which Benny sings the start of his shift at the dispatch, checking the microphone and getting into the swing of work. The song then kicks in to much more of a beat, and although Benny's vocal range becomes more wide-ranging, the song remains in speech mode. This is because its function is to convey information; speech mode does not in itself mean that the vocal line is restricted or maintains speech rhythms, much as this can also be the case and these traits can often be indications of speech mode. This song is expressive and potent with meaning in terms of Nina and Benny's first reunion within the song, but this is not the moment where these emotions take on their expression such that the song's intention is to affect. Rather, it is as if the scene of their first encounter since Nina returns home is musicalized – it feels like a musical scene, with short sung phrases between the two of them just as if they are in spoken dialogue, except it is sung. The performance mode of song gives an elevated heightening to this important moment for the two of them, but the intensification keeps its lid on and the moment remains in speech mode.

Song mode

When we say a song occurs at a higher level of emotional intensity, perhaps what we therefore mean is that song *mode* occurs at that point. Agawu describes song mode as having the quality to 'affect' (Agawu 2009, p. 99). In a musical context, this means to contain emotion, or rather to prompt an emotional response in the listener. The most obvious musical form of this might be the lyrical ballad: a song in which a character expresses their feelings on an issue. Time potentially stands still while the character explores their own personal sung monologue trying to work out or express something that they are feeling inside them. It is a personal moment, an intimate moment, an emotional moment.

'Say It Somehow' from *The Light in the Piazza* is a clear example of the performance mode of song functioning in song mode. It is in this song that Clara and Fabrizio declare their love for each other and become engaged. More than that, they express that they are able to understand each other's love in multiple forms of language and communication. The song uses traditional tropes of romantic ballads: lyrical melody lines soar with the pair of singers working together in homophonic harmony lines, moving together in the same rhythms in close harmony, before coming together in perfect unison. The harmonic language is sumptuous and the orchestration lush, prioritizing string swells and harp glissandi and passages of figuration. A significant proportion of the song has no lyrics with sung lines to 'Ah' taking over from the words which has dramatic significance given the lyrics that state their ways of communication, also giving a pure vowel sound with which to soar through the lyricism of the vocal lines.

'Say It Somehow' is a classic example of song being in song mode: it is beautiful, romantic and affecting in its soaring quality. However, the function to 'affect' can have a vast array of emotions that might be expressed.

'Waving Through a Window' from *Dear Evan Hansen* is musically an upbeat pop-style song which we might assume has taken on dance mode;

however, I would argue that this is in song mode. The song is a personal, inner monologue for Evan; despite being physically surrounded by people on his first day at a new high school, it is an expression of his inner thoughts. The drive of the music points to Evan's inner frustration at not being seen and heard or able to outwardly express himself in the way that he longs for. The vocal line of the chorus reveals the expressive person inside himself that he is not able to show and the placing of where the vocal melody sits on the hook requires a confidence of voice that belies the lack of confidence that he demonstrates outwardly. The music gives the audience a privileged insight into the kind of person that Evan is inside. Evan is affected during this song – it is an outburst of his emotions in that way. The audience is also affected emotionally by the song. The gloriousness of the song in full flight and the drive that it creates serve to rally the audience to root for Evan and long for him to show this version of himself in public.

In a similar vein 'For Forever' remains in song mode; the song is affecting on multiple levels. While this song sits slightly more in balladic territory, it remains driving in its rhythmic orchestration and does not fall into the more self-evident world of balladic writing as for example in 'Requiem'. Song mode is created through other means. In a similar turn of melodic phrasing to 'Waving Through a Window' there is a climb up to a melodic phrase peak which then retracts back down again. This shape is repeated over and over again, giving a sense of waves of yearning. There is, similarly to the earlier song, a sense of glorious release to the song, playing again on the sense that Evan finds expressive release as a character through it. We get the impression that Evan would never have been able to express this through his spoken means of communication; the song allows him expression and this in itself is affecting. In a diegetic sense – meaning in the characters' reality – the song is intended to affect Connor's family. Evan's intention is for this moment to be an affecting one where they are able to start to believe that Connor had benevolent qualities and a meaningful friendship. For the audience, the song has an additional layer of affecting because they know that what is being expressed is not true. For the audience there are two layers of emotional affect: the strength of support within the friendship Evan is recounting; and the audience's knowledge that this level of friendship does not really exist in Evan's life.

Both of these examples from *Dear Evan Hansen* show that song mode does not have to be achieved through slow tempo, highly lyrical balladic style. They also demonstrate that dramatic context provides additional layers of emotional engagement. Irony can be a profound tool, such as that being used here in the fact that Evan can be so emotional engaging and expressive in song mode, when the thought that he is not contributes to what torments him so much. This invokes even more empathy for him. It is interesting to note that the majority of the songs in *Dear Evan Hansen* are in song mode; most of the songs in the musical have the intention of affecting emotionally. This makes sense dramaturgically because the entire show is predicated around Evan's emotional well-being and the journey that he goes through hoping to being seen, heard and accepted. It is an affecting show on many levels with themes of depression, anxiety, suicide and the power of love and friendship. To be moved by the show, and for it to make the audience think more on its themes, are important, and song mode seems appropriate for a piece such as this. Variety is achieved through changes in feel, often locking into a feel-good singer-songwriter vibe, which in the film version becomes particularly pertinent due to the discovery of the video of Connor's final diegetic song in this style. The pitfall of a show that is mostly in song mode, as we have discussed, is that it becomes too much of a wash, and the rhythmic precision and flow of the stylistic choices and shifts ensure that this does not become the case in *Dear Evan Hansen*, holding the more expressive, lyrical, balladic style for the last part of the musical (see further discussion of this on p. 112). Modes of enunciation can really help this kind of consideration when creating a musical. Of the songs that occur in the film version of *Dear Evan Hansen* (the stage version has some additional songs) it is perhaps only 'Sincerely Me' which has a different mode of enunciation: dance mode.

Dance mode

Dance mode is characterized by Agawu as rhythmic; a moment that sets your internal metronome ticking. This can also be for narrative reasons. All musicals need drive at certain points – an injection of energy, something that shifts from lyricism, that surprises perhaps, that pounds or throbs with danger, or sparkles with comedy. Such a rhythmic impetus might imply a heightening of stakes, a threat of danger of some kind, a final cumulation of tension exploding. Or it might be an eruption of narrative-driven joyful exuberance.

Whilst we saw the score for *Dear Evan Hansen* is mostly in song mode, the score for *The Secret Diary of Adrian Mole Aged 13$^{3/4}$* spends the larger part in dance mode. The score comprises multiple songs which inspire a rhythmic energy, using a variety of means of doing so. If we look at songs 2–4 in the progression of the show, we can see this played out. 'Look at that Girl', the first song after the opening extended musical sequence, employs an upbeat shuffle contributing to the 'bounce' and show style of the song. It is a 'number' in the sense of having an outward-facing presentational show style, growing in forces throughout the song to give a sense of climax and satisfaction in the true 'toe-tapping' sense. This style and rhythmic upbeatness, in terms of character, establishes itself as aligned with Pandora, giving her a sense of upbeat, outward-facing personality. 'Intellectual Boy' begins in speech mode with Adrian musing on his intellectual engagement with life for the first verse. Once he has the thought of sending his poetry to the BBC, the song locks into dance mode with an upbeat rhythmic drive that parallels that of Pandora, but with a straight, rather than shuffle, beat. This song puts his character in a similar soundworld to his crush, Pandora. As with the former song, it builds to include chorus vocal elements, gradually getting more and more heightened with a show-style climax. 'Begging You for More' invokes dance mode through the use of tango style and the cultural codes that brings about in terms of associations with passion, used in this context for the affair between Adrian's mother, Pauline, and her neighbour, Mr Lucas. The strong, characterized use of the tango here places the song in dance mode in a different manner to the two songs that have preceded it. 'Barry's Threat' invokes dance mode in a different way again: through drawing on rocky influences, heavy drumming and distorted chugging guitar, characterizing the bully of the piece. The interplay between the rhythmic style of the songs and the style of lyric writing contributes to the feel of dance mode. The lyrics rhyme multiply, aiding their comedy, often using short phrases in between each rhyme so that the landing of each rhyme in itself provides rhythmic bite. Dance mode works with the lyric fully enabling the comedy to land.

The primary dance mode of enunciation of *Adrian Mole* sets into relief the musical sound world of Adrian's parents' marriage crisis. Following the four songs that we have just discussed, 'Perfect Mother' is the first of the show to move into song mode, portraying the vulnerability of Pauline's feelings about her marriage. Song mode continues through the journey of their marriage through the songs 'My Lost Love' and 'I Miss Our Life', reserving this mode of enunciation for a very specific narrative thread throughout the show, set against a backdrop of dance mode, with intermittent speech mode.

Dance mode is used in *In the Heights* in both a diegetic and non-diegetic sense. The dance mode of 'In the Club' is literal, underscoring the dance of the club and the narrative of Vanessa dancing with a variety of people, with Usnavi feeling unable to join in. Within the sequence it also provides the backdrop to put into relief an emotional moment of song mode between Nina and Benny as she tries to apologize. Dance mode is also important in this sequence as it climbs and heightens in intensification of upbeat rhythmic drive before being interrupted by the blackout. This first half of the show has been progressing towards counting down to the day of blackout, and 'In the Club' is the final moment of increased drive through so that the moment of blackout, stripping everything away, is a pronounced contrast. 'Carnaval Del Barrio' also has an element of diegesis to it, deliberately trying to inspire dance mode in the community to bring them back to life from a sluggish ennui. The sequence brings about a sense of community regeneration and a carnival feel to the scene. Crucial information is also included in this scene, such as the fact Abuela Claudia's numbers won the lotto. Arguably this momentarily places the sequence in speech mode, but fleetingly, as dance mode is re-established in the celebratory response of the community to this news. Dance mode is also used as a container in a similar way in '96,000'. This is also a large company number, with dance mode invoking the rhythmic drive of the community thinking about what they would do with 96K if they won the lottery. The whole community are incited into thinking about it, just as the community is incited to celebration in 'Carnaval Del Barrio'. There are moments that feel more like speech mode as individuals have conversations about what they might do with the money. There are also moments that feel like driven song mode, such as Sonny's impassioned section about what he would do to improve the living conditions and prospects of the community, and Vanessa's lyrical cry to want to leave. Overall, the song inspires dance mode and a communal sense of drive, but this foundation allows moments in the other two modes to fuse together and create more layered shaping within the overall container. Dance mode is perhaps the mode of enunciation that can facilitate such a fusing best.

Mixing modes of enunciation

In order to create shaping in a musical we need to be employing all three modes of enunciation. If we recall Scott McMillin's thoughts cited in Chapter 5 about the 'crackle of difference' in relation to literal performance modes, the same applies for modes of enunciation. Just as that difference brought about by shifts between performance modes is needed, so too do we need the twists and turns that are brought about by modes of enunciation rubbing up against each other, and creating contrasts of mood in our emotional and physical systems. For those of us who love musicals, they send us on a journey of shifting emotions and sensations which we very often experience viscerally. As we have discussed, it is the very piling in of all of the different performance modes, visual media and differences in expression that causes us to ride the wave of the shapes being created. The job for both composer and analyst is to understand how to read these shapes of expression: for the analyst to observe them and question how and why they are being created at certain points in the musical and what meaning might be attributed to this; for the composer, to understand them such that you can create them in the first place.

Returning to our ideas of Chapter 1, it may well be that there is a narrative imperative for your show to have a particular predominant performance mode *or* mode of enunciation. Where one mode of enunciation is dominant, there needs to be all three present in order to create the contrast needed for good storytelling. If there is one dominant performance mode (e.g. your show is through-sung), then there needs to be a mean of creating all three modes of enunciation within that dominant performance mode. Otherwise, we are likely to create a wash which stays on a level without allowing us to ride the wave of storytelling.

As we have said, *The Light in the Piazza* is a show which prioritizes music and has a highly lyrical score. The show is also an emotive one, whose themes focus on unconditional love and the generational difference between expressions of love and what can go wrong. This is all emotional material. But as we have discussed, the show cannot remain in song mode throughout as it will lose emotional connection without contrasts to that nature of affect. A song such as 'Statues and Stories' is fully situated within the world of the lush orchestration and harmonic language, but the song is in speech mode to begin the show, introducing the combination of storytelling within lyricism that is found throughout the show. 'The Beauty Is' rides an alternation between speech and song mode. The first section is in speech mode as Clara externalizes her inner monologue when sightseeing and musing on the statues that she is seeing. There is then a shift as she becomes self-aware, referring to herself in a foreign country and how she is feeling. At this point the song becomes inward and changes into song mode. As she returns to observation about Italy she returns to speech mode, becoming self-reflective again and returning to song mode. There are evident shifts in musical language between these sections and it is most significant in the changes in accompanimental figures rather than in the vocal line – which itself maintains a sense of similarity of character throughout the song. The accompanimental patterns, however, shift, most fundamentally in rhythm and in complexity of intricacy. The piano reduction of the score demonstrates that in the speech mode sections the accompaniment is characterized by an intricate interplay between left and right hands, between them maintaining a consistent semi-quaver pulse, although the way that the bass and treble interrelate creates a sense of syncopation despite the consistency of rolling semi-quavers. The song mode sections are characterized by a different pattern; calmer, simpler with a more sustained bass line with chords, in a lilting form of um-cha pattern. Clara's outward-facing excitement and semi-agitation with the outside world are set against an alternation with her inner world being calmer musically and more lyrically expressive. This is an important character distinction to establish from what is essentially her 'I Want' song: these two sides to her personality – there is an agitation present and there is also a calmer sense of control which we later discover her parents have failed to see.

'Hysteria' portrays that which her parents have focused on as a lack of ability to look after herself. On losing her way in unfamiliar streets and starting to become fearful of those surrounding her Clara becomes more and more distressed. The progression of this song also demonstrates changes in mode of enunciation. As Clara sets off singing her street directions she is in speech mode, factually reciting where she is supposed to be going. The orchestration and accompaniment patterns suggest a move into dance mode with a much more jaunty repeated quaver figure giving a spring to her step as she moves through the streets. At the ends of phrases Clara's vocal line moves into her characteristic lyricism, but the song's function is still one of factually walking at this stage. These moments, however, hint at her inner emotional landscape which gradually begins to descend into turmoil. The harmony becomes increasingly dissonant, and the orchestra becomes fragmented into sudden shocks of music with silence in between, and with turbulent orchestrations. This could be seen to be a form of song mode – it has the function of affecting as Clara's emotional state escalates. When her mother finds her, a child-like lullaby is evoked, with metallic timbre remaining in dissonance to suggest at the receding horror of Clara's experience, and perhaps at the 'something-wrong-ness' of the way Margaret sees her. The song moves firmly into lyrical song mode as Margaret calms Clara as a mother comforts a child. 'Hysteria' demonstrates the use of modes of enunciation to aid the journey of a song as it charts its dramatic course. A moment need not stay in the same mode of enunciation for an entire block of time, but can shift moment by moment depending on what needs to be conveyed. As has been seen in both of these examples from *The Light in the Piazza* it does not necessarily need to be every musical element that works to the same end. Clara's vocal lines often maintain their lyricism even when she is in speech mode, with the orchestration and language of the orchestral accompaniment patterns carrying a lot of the storytelling as part of a whole picture.

The opening song of 'In the Heights' is an example of a song where all three modes of enunciation are used. It is an example of a long extended musical sequence which sets up the whole world of Washington Heights and the characters and community that we are to follow through the rest of the show. The show opens in speech mode with Usnavi speaking directly to the audience, introducing them to his world, his family history and his shop. The density of the lyrics in Usnavi's rap through the opening of the song is an indication of speech mode, but it is actually because his intention is to convey a lot of information. The sung material between Nina's parents and Usnavi as the pair come into the shop for a coffee and lottery ticket still remains in speech mode, as does the exchange between Daniela and Carla following this. Despite the change in style and vocal lyricism for Kevin's entrance, and then again for Daniela and Carla into what might be considered more of a dance rhythm, the dramatic intention for all of their short sections is to convey information to other characters – going about their daily business. This is the stuff of speech mode. The repeated company chorus arguably *does* go into dance mode, creating rhythmic drive and demonstrating the unity of the community. Three-quarters through the sequence, there is a short moment of song mode in the exchange between Vanessa and Usnavi, demonstrating the chemistry between the two of them. Returning to rap, Usnavi stays in song mode for a while with a much more impassioned section about how he feels about his living situation and history, interlayered with single soaring lines from his beloved Abuela, and the full company – this section takes on much more potency of emotional connotation – before then erupting into a final section in dance mode with the full company leading to a heightened end to the song. Predominantly this opening extended musical sequence is in speech mode, conveying large amounts of character and plot set up information to the audience throughout the changes in style and performance mode that are interwoven to keep the dynamic constantly shifting. There are then short sections of song and dance mode to give emotional and structural changes and demonstrating the range of emotional and performative modes that will be encountered throughout the whole musical. In this way the world of the musical to come is stylishly, efficiently, dramatically and characterfully established.

Summing up

The discussion in this chapter complexifies the idea of the intensification chart which we saw in Chapter 5. We have seen that the notion of shape is no longer solely down to whether the character speaks, sings or dances in the literal sense, but in some way is also determined by the mode of enunciation of the material, irrespective of its performance mode. The level of intensification of any one moment is down to a number of factors, and in some way a consideration of the amalgamation of how heightened the performance modes are, coupled with consideration of its mode of enunciation. We then still have the factor, as seen before, of how many kinds of performance mode are stacked or combined in terms of the scale of sensory heightening or overwhelm. Let's keep all of these factors in play as we move on to look at some shapes in practice.

7

Big shapes

In Chapter 5 we looked at the principle of the dynamic curve and how it relates to intensification. We have also looked at intensification in the context of both performance modes and modes of enunciation. Let's bring this together and look at the dynamic curve in practice in the context of musical theatre.

In this chapter we are going to focus on what I am calling 'big shapes'; by this I am referring to the overarching shapes brought about by the whole show, or by an act. A flat dynamic curve shape where there is little undulation of shaping is what we are trying to avoid – stasis tends to inhibit drama. As we said in Chapter 5, Agawu's basic dynamic curve shape grows to a highpoint of intensification at about the three-quarters mark in the structure, before moderately decreasing the intensification to the end. This would imply, from a composer's perspective, that if we apply this shape to the whole musical, presuming at this stage a traditional full-length two-act structure, then the musical climax would arrive at about three-quarters of the way through the show, around halfway through Act 2. Interestingly the song that occurs at this point of the show has traditionally been called the 'eleven o'clock number' and has connotations with being a big musical moment that might be a standout point in the score.

We are going to talk in generalities for a while, assuming various aspects of traditional musical theatre shapes and conventions. For now, we are going to assume: a book-musical whereby there are scenes and songs in alternation; a two-act structure; a linear narrative which includes cause and effect; a sense of a protagonist's journey in the narrative. The principles will absolutely apply to other non-traditional forms of musical theatre equally, but let's look at the standard structures before we deviate from them.

The monomyth and the dynamic curve

In his book *How Musicals Work*, Julian Woolford discusses the monomyth as a framework for charting narrative structure, which can helpfully be applied to the musical (see Woolford 2012, chapter 5). The monomyth is based on the hero's journey, a traditional storytelling structure based on a protagonist's journey through a story (see Joseph Campbell et al.). In brief, the twelve stages of the monomyth that Woolford sets out are:

1　The Ordinary World

2　Call to Adventure

3　Refusal of the Call

4　Floating Stage – Meeting the Mentor

5　Crossing the Threshold

6　Test, Allies and Enemies

7　Preparation for the Supreme Ordeal

8　The Supreme Ordeal

9　Reward

10　The Road Back

11　The Final Conflict

12　Return to Stability

(Woolford 2012, p. 105)

Let's begin by identifying the highpoint(s). The highpoint(s) would seem to be important markers in the shape that you are creating. As we have seen, they can be identified as the moments of most intensity narratively, and the highest level of intensity in terms of performance mode, also taking into consideration the mode of enunciation that you might want to use to convey that particular narrative unit. The highpoint for Agawu is a 'superlative moment' (2009, p. 46) of heightened intensity. The superlative nature of the highpoint indicates the importance of an intensification of affect, brought about at salient points within a work. In his method it is the placing of highpoints within a whole work which creates a shape to the piece which can be represented in the form of the curve. Agawu's highpoint provides a framework by which the consideration of the shape of each musical can be realized. According to Agawu, a highpoint is defined as:

> a moment of great intensity, a point of extreme tension, or the site of a decisive release of tension. It usually marks a turning point in the form … Psychologically, a single highpoint typically dominates a single composition, but given the fact that a larger whole is often constituted by smaller parts, each of which might have its own intensity curve, the global highpoint may be understood as a product of successive local highpoints. Because of its marked character, the highpoint may last a moment, but it may also be represented as an extended moment – a plateau or region.
>
> (Agawu 2009, p. 62)

Based on this definition, in the monomyth, the highpoints would seem to be at stage 7 (The Supreme Ordeal) and stage 11 (The Final Conflict). These moments of ordeal or conflict can be seen as the most intense – a form of climax. In the monomyth these occur just either side of the three-quarter marker we were discussing. If we refer back to Agawu's basic dynamic curve in Chapter 5, the highpoint there would seem to match most closely to The Final Conflict, before tailoring off to stage 12 (Return to Stability). There are other moments of intensity along the way that lead to The Final Conflict, most notably The Supreme Ordeal, and so the basic dynamic curve shape starts to take on more undulations. The monomyth might be conceptualized by a gradual climb through stages 1–3; a potential lowering around stages 3–4, before climbing again from 5 through to 8; a lowering through 9–10 and then another climb for stage 11, and a lowering to resolution at 12. This results in:

Hill (1–3)
Shallow valley/plateau (3–4)
Hill (5–8)
Shallow valley (9–10)
Steep hill (11)
Valley (12)

If we sketch out an approximation of this shape, we can see that it has a few more twists along the way than the basic dynamic curve shape. Let's look at the narrative shaping of *Matilda*, which is a two-act book musical with a traditional form of structuring.

Stage of the Monomyth	Narrative unit in *Matilda*
1. The Ordinary World	Matilda is born and rejected by her parents. Five years later they refuse to see her genius.
2. Call to Adventure	Matilda has to start school.
3. Refusal of the Call	Not applicable – while her parents do not care if Matilda goes to school, there is no refusal of this from Matilda.
4. Floating Stage, Meeting the Mentor	Matilda meets her teacher Miss Honey who functions as her Mentor.
5. Crossing the Threshold	This could be the first day of school, or more likely it could be her first encounter with Miss Trunchbull.
6. Tests, Allies and Enemies	A series of cruel encounters at school with Trunchbull, including Bruce being dragged to chokey.
7. Preparation for the Supreme Ordeal	Matilda decides she will bring an end to Trunchbull's cruelty. Lavender puts a newt in Trunchbull's water jug.
8. The Supreme Ordeal	Through being able to move objects with her mind, Matilda mentality knocks over the water jug with the newt onto Trunchbull.
9. Reward	Miss Honey invites Matilda for tea.
10. The Road Back	At home, Miss Honey tells Matilda of her family background and situation, and reveals her modest living conditions.

Stage of the Monomyth	Narrative unit in *Matilda*
11. The Final Conflict	Matilda uses her powers to write ghostly messages on the blackboard, getting rid of Miss Trunchbull forever.
12. Return to Stability	Miss Honey becomes headmistress of the school and Matilda lives with her as her unloving family move to Spain.

I am not suggesting that the writers of *Matilda* actively charted the narrative through in this way; it is more that such patterns of narrative structure exist in a lot of storytelling – hence the studies of Joseph Campbell, and Woolford's ability to discuss musical theatre within the terms of these patterns. We can see that the narrative of *Matilda* does demonstrate correlation with the outline sketch of the narrative dynamic curve of the monomyth.

Understanding the narrative shape of your show is important for the composer. What you now do with this information creatively is a different matter. It might be that you are trying to chart the same dynamic curve, highlighting narrative moments of greatest intensity with musical moments of greatest intensity. This is one way to approach the score; highlighting with music the intrinsic narrative shape of the show which is brought about by the plot. However, if we look at the score for *Matilda*, the two points that we have said are the highpoints – the two occasions on which *Matilda* takes on Miss Trunchbull secretly by using her telekinetic powers – both occur during book time. These are not the big sung musical numbers in the show. 'Chalk Writing' is the musical moment surrounding the ghostly writing on the board that finally dispatches Miss Trunchbull. However, this occurs through underscored dialogue. The number that follows, 'Revolting Children', is the celebratory number that follows Miss Trunchbull's departure, and is indeed a heightened number in terms of forces, rhythm, orchestration and texture. However, this is narratively more related to the Return to Stability – the victory – than the actual conflict itself. 'Quiet' is the song that happens closest to Matilda's first triumph over Miss Trunchbull involving the newt and the water jug. This song is striking for its simplistic beauty: after the tumultuous opening to the song, the portrayal of quiet is powerful in its internalized beauty. Different approaches to the highpoint will be discussed further below, but this is perhaps not immediately what might be expected musically for this moment when looking at the dynamic curve of the narrative structure.

But this is only surprising if one were trying to follow the dynamic curve of the narrative with the musical intensification. This is perhaps the approach that might be taken on a piece which is more akin to a 'play with songs', where the book is dictating the narrative structure, and the song points highlight these moments. However, another approach is that the score is such an intrinsic part of the process that the songs don't chart the narrative shape – as if something were there already that the music is following – but rather the music is so inherent to the process that it is creating part of the shape in the first place. The presence of the score in a musical completely changes the dynamic curve of the show as a whole, when compared with the dynamic curve of the narrative alone. Let's remember here the difference between story and plot. The *story* that you are trying to tell will already have its own shape that is perhaps inevitable. But the *plot*, the way you are telling that story, is all up for grabs and that shape is likely to be a different shape to the story. It's important that the whole team have collectively decided on the music's role in creating that shape and whether the songs are a part of *making* that shape, or whether they are *following* that shape.

In *Matilda*, some of the standout song moments are not moments that are found to be the most intense in the narrative. Instead, the score creates further undulations in the dynamic curve of the show as a whole. One such example is 'When I Grow Up' which functions as a thematic song in the musical. It is not related to any particular plot moment, but instead stands as a statement of the children's hopes and dreams, set against the backdrop of the terror of the Trunchbull in the context of the wider show. The song is also an important structural marker; it opens Act 2, and its reprise closes the show, in combination with reprise 2 of 'Naughty'. This is an important consideration. The traditional book musical has particular structural moments that usually require heightening, typically the beginnings and endings of acts. In fact, the opening of Act 2 in *Matilda* has two songs which stand outside the literal narrative. First, 'Telly' creates the energetic, comedic opening of Act 2 which Mr Wormwood addresses directly to the audience, commending watching TV to them. This functions as an audience settler, reminding the audience of Matilda's family context, and taking the audience back into the world of the show. 'When I Grow Up' is then a moment of pathos where we are given a privileged insight into the inner feelings of the children, which are not conveyed in the action of the show. This takes on the guise of an anthem to freedom; dreaming of the possibilities beyond the gates of school, rules and restrictions. While the audience receives this against the context of their life at school with Miss Trunchbull, it is as if it could be a wider anthem applicable to life beyond the show, until Miss Honey's solo section, leading into the duet with Matilda's counter-melody from 'Naughty' takes us right back into the specificity of the context where we had left the show at the end of Act 1. This whole section functions outside of the literal narrative storytelling, but is so important in the shape of the show. Reconnecting with the world of the show following an interval is a transition that has to be navigated by the writers, and *Matilda's* score achieves it in stages: first functioning quasi non-diegetically with Mr Wormwood, taking us a step further into the diegesis with the children, and then arriving fully back in the diegesis of the show with Miss Honey and Matilda. In terms of the dynamic curve of the show, this has created an additional high region before gradually drawing us back and down the curve into the action.

'The Smell of Rebellion' is also a big number which is character driven, rather than related to one of the important narrative beats in the show listed in the table of narrative units on p. 106. This song is important in character portrayal regarding Trunchbull. Its most important function, however, is perhaps one of tone. The song is a big number which takes multiple twists and turns and contrasts of style, all against the visuals of the children doing their gruelling 'phys ed' lesson. The song is funny, and truly a character song in that it both gives us further insight into the workings of Trunchbull's mind, and also in the sense of being a comedy character number. This sets a certain Roald Dahl-esqe tone for the Trunchbull; she becomes the villain that we love to hate as opposed to the show becoming a truly dark story. Again, this number creates a heightened, almost show-stopping, moment where there is not a moment of heightened intensity in the narrative units. Again, the score re-draws the dynamic curve of the show, and complexifies it far beyond the basic shapes that we have looked at. This process, of the score (and other choreographic, visual and artistic factors) crafting the dynamic curve, and thereby the shaping of the whole show, reveals one of the things that is so exciting about musical theatre. The charting of intensification in a multifaceted, multidisciplinary way and the continual heightening and releasing of intensity – beyond what the story alone would be – is one of the art form's characteristics, and part of what makes being a musical theatre composer such an exciting undertaking.

Complexifying the use of the dynamic curve

While the pattern of the dynamic curve discussed above is the basic shape of the concept, as we have just seen there are limitless different dynamic shapes that are possible; shapes that can be seen as representational of the form of the work. Agawu suggests that the '[p]arameters that define this basic shape differ from work to work' (Agawu 2009, p. 62) and the appropriate definition of what constitutes a highpoint needs to be explored in each context. Not only can the parameters be defined according to the appropriate focus in question at any one time, but they can also be applied on differing levels of scale from conceptualizing the whole show through to an individual moment (as we will do in Chapter 8).

At the level of literal performance modes, the intensification chart on p. 83 suggests a particular set of parameters by which the highpoints could be defined in a musical; from a perspective of heightening of performance mode, those moments at level D could be argued to be the highpoints of the musical, with level A as the lower points and level B and C as interim points in between. Thus, the shape of the intensification chart we looked at previously could be seen to equate to the dynamic shape to be analysed in Agawu's terms. However, as we have already noted, the moments of level D in performance intensification (from the perspective of heightening of performance modes) do not necessarily equate with the moments that would be identified as emotionally intense, and it is those moments of emotional intensity that would seem to align themselves more with the spirit of Agawu's concept of the highpoint. As we have seen, intensification of narrative is not necessarily where we find intensification of performance mode. We have also seen that intensification of performance mode does not necessarily equate with heightening of emotional moment. When used in combination with consideration of modes of enunciation, a more detailed picture can be sought. For example, song mode suggests a greater intensity of affect than the other two modes, and so a moment of entering song mode may be seen as more significant in terms of reaching highpoint status than the literal performance mode of song. It seems as if we are caught in a bit of a 'catch-22' situation here in terms of how we identify the highpoints in the musical, or decide where they should occur. Let's not forget that there is no 'should' about it: Agawu's work reminds us that the parameters must be set by each creative or analyst, according to their particular purposes.

Dear Evan Hansen, like *Matilda*, is also a two-act book musical. Defining the dynamic curves of the show in different ways provides interesting insights into the various shapes occurring in the show. As we saw in Chapter 6, the large majority of the songs in *Dear Evan Hansen* are in song mode of enunciation: it is a show which has the function to 'affect' for a large proportion of the piece. However, for this to be the case, variety has to be obtained in one way or another because otherwise that level of emotion cannot be sustained over the period of an entire show. If we set the parameters of the dynamic curve to measure Evan's well-being over the course of the show we might result in: a low start, which dips further as he starts the new high school and in his encounters with Connor, followed by a slow increase (of a kind) as he befriends Zoe's family, becomes friends with Alana, becomes an internet sensation and becomes a couple with Zoe. There is a sharp plummet as the truth of his lies is revealed, and by the end of the show his well-being has increased to the highest it has been in the show due to his authenticity and integrity, revealed through his final letter to himself.

This is therefore:
Low start, and then further valley
Steady climb of the hill over a protracted period of time
Steep plummet to valley
Gradual incline to the highest point in the show.

The highest point of Evan's well-being would therefore be the ending of the show, with other high points being his speech at the memorial and the moment when he starts a relationship with Zoe.

However, this is not the same dynamic curve of the musical score. If we look at the score from the perspective of intensity brought about through upbeat tempo and rhythmic drive, it almost does a broad inverse of this curve. The first four songs of the show are the most upbeat and driving in the show – it is infused with energy through the first part of the musical despite Evan's vulnerability at the start of the piece. This intensity of drive of the first sections of the show starts to loosen at 'Requiem'. It is the ending of the show that is so interesting in terms of the lyricism and intimacy which characterize the last few songs in the musical, meaning that the show ends on a poignancy of Evan's well-being, rather than a celebratory note. The dynamic curves brought about in this way by the score in the stage version and the film version differ significantly. The removal of the highly driven song 'Good For You' and the insertion of Connor's ballad 'A Little Closer' mean that the move to lyricism happens much earlier in the film version and there is a substantial part of the final quarter of the film that is musically lyrical. Evan's turn to truth, and the feeling that he has a new start, is characterized through musical intimacy rather than heightened forms of musical language.

We can use the dynamic curve to look at this from a totally different point of view, and that is to chart the levels of *anguish* in the show. In this instance, logically enough, the dynamic curve would be turned on its head and inverted from that relating to Evan's well-being. The show narrative therefore starts at quite a high level of intensity, which becomes increasingly intense through Evan's being bullied and this seems reflected in the level of drive of the score. To look at the other end of the show, the drive and power of 'Good For You' creates a heightening around the moment of discovering Evan's lies, reflecting the anguish of his family and friends. 'Words Fail' then stands out being brought about by stripping this drive away, leaving Evan musically vulnerable in his outpouring at this point. This is mirrored by Heidi's vulnerability in 'So Big/So Small'. This whole high region narratively of anguish of multiple parties is stripped away to intimacy in a musical sense. The dynamic curve relating to anguish then falls to a low level for the end of the show. Because of the particular storyline of *Dear Evan Hansen*, the Return to Stability here is much more pronounced. It is not really a 'return' to stability but rather a much more significant finding of a new stability where there was none before. The intimate lyrical ending musically therefore creates a dynamic curve which gives poignancy to an ending, leaving an audience on an exhale rather than a high. We can see that the parameters of the dynamic curve can be changed to give the viewpoint that is most helpful: it could be that it is a helpful tool to put a certain theme under the spotlight for example, and chart through the shaping of a theme in terms of intensification over time. From whichever viewpoint, the dynamic curve of *Dear Evan Hansen* can be seen to differ from the basic dynamic curve shape, particularly as regards its opening and ending regions. This is the shape that arises from telling this particular story in this way.

Types of highpoint

To return to Agawu's definition, there are three guidelines given in terms of identifying potential highpoints:

1   'A point of extreme tension,'

2   'the site of a decisive release of tension,'

3   'a turning point in the form'. (Agawu 2009, p. 62)

Given the methods which have already been explored, the idea of accumulation as regards the highpoint and points of extreme tension is a useful one: we can create extreme tension narratively, through performance mode or through mode of enunciation, or the combination of these factors. It is very interesting to the context of a musical score that this tension can seemingly be accumulated, as in Agawu's definition 1, or 'released' as in definition 2. This makes sense to us in the context of singing where tension is often released through song. Continuing to look at *Dear Evan Hansen*, the song 'Words Fail' could be seen as an example of this kind of moment. All of the tension that Evan has accumulated through the show, as his lies have escalated, pours out of him in this song. The song builds throughout getting more impassioned in a musical and vocal release of emotion. 'Words Fail' is not the 'biggest' song in the show, but it is perhaps the most primal outpouring of emotion in the show. Definition 3, 'a turning point in the form', also serves as a useful idea, functioning on two levels in the context of the musical: Agawu suggests this within the context of the structural form of a piece of music, and it can certainly be applied in this way to the musical's component parts. We saw how the beginning of Act 2 of *Matilda* serves as a high point because of a turning point in the form *of the musical.* However, a turning point can also be defined dramatically in the musical in terms of narrative, coinciding with the idea of narrative reversal: the moment at which the plot, or a character's journey, takes a new turn. Agawu discusses how a moment of narrative reversal is of 'rhetorical significance' (Agawu 1984, p. 161) and can therefore often take on the mantle of a highpoint.

We have seen that there are different situations that create a highpoint, and we have also seen that there are multiple ways of creating one, with the defining parameters being able to be selected according to the context. In order to use the tool fully, it is not sufficient to simply state that a point is 'high' or otherwise; there are significant differences between certain types of highpoint. I propose that it's helpful to extend our thinking on this a little further and conceptualize four different ways of bringing about a highpoint. The examples below are all songs, because we are focusing on the composer's role, but this is not to imply that highpoints are always brought about by song – these types of moments could equally occur through dialogue or movement.

The highpoint of intensity

This is perhaps the form of highpoint we would think of first – a moment of high intensity brought about by a particular heightening of action. An example of this is 'Blackout' from *In the Heights*, brought about by the extreme situation of blackout across the city that the show has been building up to until this point. It is exacerbated further by the multiple different points of view and strands of storytelling going on simultaneously, resulting in multiple musical strands occurring in polyphony – overlapping melodies which all combine in their interplay. The number is also heightened in terms of its thick vocal texture, rhythmic orchestration and epic style.

The highpoint of lyricism

We have already seen 'Words Fail' as an example of this from *Dear Evan Hansen*: a moment of emotional outpouring, often taking place in song. 'Still Hurting' from *The Last Five Years* – Cathy's expression of intense devastation at the breakdown of her marriage – is another example.

The highpoint of spectacle

This is a highpoint in the form rather than in the narrative. This is closely related to intensification of performance modes, and to Siropoulos's ideas relating to audiovisual overwhelm. There are a few examples in *In the Heights*: '96,000' is one example of this kind of spectacle of multiple performance modes in a heightened, big 'number'. 'Carnaval Del Barrio' is another example, and is an example of how this can also function narratively as there are various strands of storytelling that occur through this sequence. 'Revolting Children', discussed above, is also an example of this kind of highpoint brought about by spectacle and size.

The highpoint of intimacy

This is a highpoint whose significance is brought about by its quality of intimacy rather than its largesse. It does the opposite of what one might initially expect – rather than grow to an intense statement, everything is stripped away. 'Quiet' from *Matilda* that we looked at above is an example of this – it stands out because of its minimalism compared with everything that occurs around it.

Exposition and development

It has been seen that Agawu focuses on the shape of a work created by focusing on its highpoints, however, we can't just categorize moments simply into those that are high, and those that are not. What about the moments on the way up and down; the climbs in between a 'resting' point and 'high' points? If the highpoint is taken to be a superlative moment, I propose that two stages before this are useful to demonstrating shape. These can be referred to as 'exposition' and 'development'. When a unit of narrative has a status of exposition, this relates to the conveyance of information. This has echoes with how we were discussing speech mode in the previous chapter.

'Phoning Home' and 'Costume Party' from *Come From Away* is an example of a sequence of exposition. Throughout the number, various members of the people on the planes make phone calls to family and we gradually get to know more about the new arrivals to Newfoundland. They form an extended musical sequence, where the entirety moves between underscored dialogue and song, moving the story along as we follow multiple people's narratives through the sequence. 'Passeggiata' from *The Light in the Piazza* might be another example. This is a simpler version, where the whole song is a simpler moment between just two characters – Clara and Fabrizio. In terms of narrative function, they are simply going for a walk around the city. From a character perspective, it is an important meeting moment that starts the beginnings of their relationship. As we have seen, much of the score for the show is lyrical, so it is not that the song is less expressive than others in the show, but the function is one of introduction of their relationship to each other, with a calm situation and lack of stakes at this point.

Material which is 'development' has a higher level of intensification than exposition, but is not yet at the status of a highpoint. It might be that when a curve shape is growing, it is a region of development. It's helpful to think of development as 'dwelling on something'. An idea has been established, perhaps earlier in the show, and it is now being developed – the character is trying to decide what to do about something; or tensions might be building or the knot tightening over a particular issue. '38 Planes' from *Come From Away* is a good example of this. It is an extended musical sequence, involving underscored dialogue as well as song, developing the situation that has been established in the opening number. The choral vocal element to this is important in tightening the knot of development; the insistence of the repetition of the choral vocals sitting beneath the dialogue keeps the curve of tension rising. 'On the Edge' is another example from the same show; the function of the moment is to keep the tension rising, moving in and out of speech and song as the disasters of the situation continue to escalate.

The musicologists among you will recognize the language of 'exposition' and 'development' as relevant to classical musical structures; sonata form for example. The dramatists among you will recognize the term 'exposition' in terms of things that we need to learn in a dramatic plot. While the terms are being re-contextualized here, these meanings are still helpful. Common to all of them is a lower-intensity level of establishing something for the first time, and then a higher, or growing level of intensity of working something out, developing an idea, spinning a theme; a process of elaboration. Of course, what makes this a trickier concept is that the establishment of the theme might be intense: a show might start with an explosion; the music of the opening might be dramatic, forceful and thick in texture. Perhaps in these moments the show in fact starts on a highpoint and the exposition (or explanation of it) comes later when the heat is lowered. In other words, exposition and establishing doesn't have to come first. However, think of 'Ex-Wives', the opening number of *Six* which starts in an explosion of musical intensity, but also contains the establishing storytelling of the show amidst it – this simultaneously has a function of exposition and also starting on a highpoint.

In fact, there is a typical trope of musical theatre in which the opening number is an extended sequence where multiple characters are introduced and the whole world of the show is established within the one number. These kinds of opening numbers do a lot of work in terms of literal exposition, but they are often big numbers and so might be providing a dual function: a highpoint of spectacle but with a narrative function of exposition. 'Ex-Wives' is one such example, as is 'Miracle' from *Matilda*, 'Welcome to the Rock' from *Come From Away* and 'In the Heights' from the show of the same name.

Non-book musicals

We said at the beginning of this chapter that we were going to look at traditional structures to begin with, so let's move away from that now and look at the example of *35MM*. Ryan Scott Oliver's *35MM* does not have a narrative which is overarching to the whole show. It is a concept musical, or could be referred to a song cycle, whereby four characters perform the sequence of songs, not maintaining one character throughout, but rather each song is in itself an individual story. The show is inspired by a collection of photographs by Matthew Murphey, and so each song is self-contained, pertaining to one photograph. There are linking sections – 'Transitions' – and numbers which allude to the very nature of photography itself as a medium. The musical itself has the strap line 'A Musical Exhibition', presenting itself as the equivalent of a curated exhibition of photographs. The songs are somehow simultaneously entirely individual and stand alone, and yet part of a whole. A piece like *35MM* functions in a totally different way to the book musical, and resists any kind narrative structuring of cause and effect. How then can shaping and the dynamic curve relate to this, or be useful in this regard?

We will see in the next chapter, that the dynamic curve is particularly helpful when looking at the smaller-scale stories contained in each song in a show structure such as this. However, it is also a tool that is still helpful from the perspective of the big shape; of the show overall. It is not, probably, that narrative is the starting point for such a shape, but the musical still functions by increasing and releasing tension and creating a very tangible shape in doing so. Indeed, if anything, these contrasts and undulations of shape are needed even more due to the audience *not* following a narrative. In a show such as this, the art form itself becomes one of the most helpful parameters to chart with a dynamic curve, according to the tightening of the knot created by the music, and then the places where that is released. Indicators such as rhythmic drive, speed, the quality of timbre of the orchestration, extremes of range or serenity of smoothness of musical phrasing are just some of the parameters which might help to indicate whether the tension is being increased or lowered.

The first three songs of the show gradually climb such a dynamic curve, peaking at 'On Monday' before lowering for 'Caralee' and lowering again for 'The Party Goes With You'. There continues to be an ongoing undulation up and down of intensification over the course of the show, systematically increasing and releasing tension musically to chart a conceptual kind of shape and journey for the audience. The lowest point of this is 'Mama, Let Me In', stripped of any orchestration with sustained a capella vocals in harmony.

There is a steep climb to a peak for the next song 'Why Must We Tell Them Why?' and then another drop through the two songs following this. It could be argued that the highpoint of the whole show is the two ending numbers, and that all the undulations in between are creating a journey through to 'Sara Berry' being the peak of the show. This would make sense in a non-narrative piece where the show needs to keep propelling through to the end without the aid of narrative structuring. Song cycles such as *35MM* are difficult to write; the tools that we are discussing in this book become *more* relevant and vital rather than less, because so much of the dramaturgy is being brought about by the songs. The way they are implemented is perhaps what differs because the creative's focus of attention is a little different to the way that a book musical works.

Summing up

We have seen that the dynamic curve is, indeed, a dynamic tool in as much as it is not possible to pin down one way of exactly how one should use it. However, it is an extremely useful tool to both creative and analyst in conceptualizing what is going on with different parameters of the musical in order to ascertain shaping and how the accumulation and release of tension is mapped across the musical. We have all the tools we need to start sketching shapes to create to, or to analyse – considering the shape of the story that we are trying to tell, working out how this shape might differ to our plot shape, deciding the function of music within this shape-drawing, and using the terminology of exposition, development, highpoints, performance modes and modes of enunciation in whatever ways help to conceptualize the relationship between types of intensification building and releasing over time. These shapes of build and release are the building blocks of drama.

8
Small shapes

The shaping tools we have been looking at, the dynamic curve, performance modes and modes of enunciation, are equally helpful for creating small shapes as much as large structural shapes. By small shapes, I am referring to song shapes, the way that a song integrates with the scene around it and the shaping of that, right down to the level of individual musical phrase shapes.

Song shapes

You may be familiar with standard song structures: AAA (so-called strophic form), AABA form or the various verse-chorus forms and their derivations, perhaps using a bridge or changing whether there is a final verse or simply a final chorus, perhaps having a pre-chorus section. But why dramaturgically speaking should we use any of these structures? Sondheim famously said that 'content dictates form' (Mordden 2015 p.22), and this is a mantra which is repeated a lot in musical theatre circles. Simply, it means that the drama should dictate what forms and structures we use.

Strophic form (AAA)

In its simplest version, AAA form indicates an idea which gets repeated without much, if any, variation on that idea. The dynamic curve, certainly in terms of the music for such a form, may well be a flat line because nothing changes – an idea is set and then it repeats. We have said that we are trying to avoid flat lines, and I would suggest when it comes to big shapes that holds fast. But when it comes to small shapes, perhaps we can start to think about when flat shapes are useful. Is the character stuck in the same pattern day after day? Are they waiting for some kind of event to happen, or for inspiration to strike? In these instances, a flat dynamic curve may be exactly the song shape that is required. It is usual in musical theatre that it is desirable for the character to have moved on conceptually and arrived somewhere else in their thinking by the end of the song than they were at the beginning. Again, this helps to avoid flat-line syndrome, and also helps to avoid the kind of scenario where songs are relegated to the position of adding decoration and entertainment before we 'get back to the real stuff of the storytelling in the book'. There are, of course types of musico-dramatic forms where the songs *do* stand outside of the book and provide a comment on what is going on and when this is done purposefully it can be incredibly effective; I am merely talking about not accidentally landing in a place where the songs are not dramaturgically vital. But back to our character moving on – perhaps the very point of a moment dramaturgically speaking is that they *can't* move on, and in this scenario then we might choose the AAA shaping for that reason.

Strophic form has associations with genres such as folk music, or hymns, where it is standard that the same music is sung with different lyrics in each stanza. Sometimes in folk structures, or in the medieval forms of balladic storytelling that used strophic forms, there is a short refrain which functions a little like a chorus but shorter. 'The Tale of Solomon Snell' from *Whisper House* (by Duncan Sheik) is an example of this kind of form. It is a stand-alone story which unfolds through the song, and it is quite a close example of strophic form in the medieval balladic sense where the repeated music serves to allow the singer to tell the story bit by bit. The refrain punctuates after a few A sections, repeating the same lyrics each time. In 'Solomon Snell' the song remains in the same key, with the same feel and orchestration throughout, very much evoking the balladic style that fits the dramatic scenario of telling the tale, as the opening lines of the song directly allude to.

The influence of AAA form can also be seen in 'Screech In' from *Come From Away*. Much of the score of the show is rooted in folk style, but at this moment it is as if the diegesis is crossed such that they are singing in the bar. It is a moment where traditional customs such as 'kissing the fish' are performed in order for the plane people to become Newfoundlanders. Spirits are high, and it is a celebratory moment of togetherness that recounts folk traditions, in combination with the bar as one natural setting of folk music of this kind. The song is not, in fact, an example of the narrative standing still, as was suggested above as a possible dramaturgical use of strophic form. Instead, it is used here because it makes dramatic sense stylistically. It is the action in the song, and what the song stands for that are important in this moment, rather than revelation through song itself. The celebration of community, the release of tension of the characters and the development of the relationship between Diana and Nick are the important dramatic features of the song. Musically, other parameters are used, rather than contrasts in new musical themes, in order to create movement. One of these is tonality; there are multiple modulations in the song, taking the musical stanza on a journey of different keys which creates a sense of energy and movement. Second, the orchestration continues to evolve, and there is significant use of 'stops' – moments where everything stops for a certain number of beats before picking up again, all in time with the beat of the song – to provide rhythmic punctuation. There are underscore and instrumental versions of the melody that are played, and different arrangements of the basic thematic material. Vocally, there is a lot of rhythmic speech in storytelling guise in the song, in between sung refrains, and so even though the sung material is the same melody each time, it has been broken up by underscored rhythmic speech and variety. The sung material when it returns also changes in arrangement, creating different layers of harmony. Furthermore, three-quarters of the way through the song there is an underscore version of a section from 'Welcome to the Rock' which sets up a loop over which the action continues, before erupting into a final round of the strophic folk tune. Strictly speaking, this is therefore not quite an AAA song. However, it is certainly influenced by the strophic approach and is a good example of seeing how strophic form can be used still with dramatic shaping; this song is far from a flat dynamic curve.

AABA

Of course the music and the lyrics can have different implied shaping. Just because the music is repeating itself doesn't mean that the lyrics are also on a flat dynamic curve shape. There may be a dramatic scenario in which the music needs to keep repeating while the lyrics move us on. Often the AABA form is discussed in terms that the 'B' section helps the character think in a different way about the issue they are singing about – the music, metre and lyrics change here to shed new light on the situation. When the final A musically returns, then invariably the lyrics indicate that there has been a sense of moving on. We might ask, why then does the music remain the same? Part of the answer, I'm sure, to this question is about completeness and rounding off in a musical sense. Outside of the musico-dramatic form, returning to the original musical material is something that gives a satisfying sense of shape. If we consider the basic dynamic curve shape, then it correlates very neatly with the classic AABA structure – it rises due to a change of play and development in the B section, three-quarters of the way through the song, and then returns back down again with a sense of finishing off and completion. We can, of course, choose to return musically, or not to return. If the change of heart is so great that we feel compelled for the music to continue to move on, then this we can do, and enter into the realms of through-composing, where the music continues to evolve as and when needed and dictated by the dramatic circumstance (see below for discussion of through-composed forms). There are, however, degrees of return. The same theme could be returned to but differently – there might be a change of tonality, a change of orchestration or accompanimental pattern, perhaps even bringing about a change in effort (in the Laban or character sense).

'Stop the World' from *Come From Away* is an example of an AABA song which makes sense shape-wise of the dramatic moment involved. Nick and Diana are together, sightseeing, aware that their fledgling relationship may be about to change when they leave Gander. They are together in the moment, but the sections they sing demonstrate the individual thoughts in their heads. In this dramatic scenario, AABA works because for each of the section A's it allows for, first Nick's thoughts to be heard, and then the second A allows for Diana's thoughts to be revealed. The B section then enables them to sing together – still in their own heads – but the audience see them united in their desire for their relationship to continue after going their separate ways. The form is then truncated though – they do not reach a final full statement of A, but rather the song ends on the hook line which opens the A section. This, perhaps, is dramaturgical indication of the fact that this part of their story is not resolved. The final A section in an AABA form often gives new direction, or a sense of resolution or rounding off of the thought process that the song has contained. Here there is none, but rather the hook *is* the rounding off of their thought – stopping the world *is* where their desires are at in this moment.

'Inutil' from the stage version of *In the Heights* does exactly the same thing for dramaturgical reasons. In the first A section Kevin looks back to the past at his history with his father who considered his life choices useless. The second A section enables a contrast to be established with his pride for his daughter and how he wants her to thrive. The repetition of the same music but with different lyrics sets these two time periods against each other, establishing the link between them in Kevin's mind. The B section then reiterates his determination that he will not repeat the mistakes of his father, and the song ends with this statement of defiance and resilience, spurring the narrative onwards, rather than suggesting the resolution that returning to the A section would imply.

The dynamic curve shape for both of these songs would remain at a moderate level through both of the A sections, and then would indicate a step up for the start of the B section and a curve upwards through that, finishing the song at the heightened level without the lowering of intensification of a return. 'Stop the World' creates a small rounding off of the dynamic curve through musical means of stripping back the texture, including a vocal rit (slowing down) and a gentle placing of the final word. 'Inutil', however, maintains the high level of intensity to the very end.

Verse-chorus

Verse-chorus patterns perhaps give us both a feeling of stasis as seen in AAA form, but with a range of flexibility for development and growth where required. Verse-chorus inherently suggests there are two things going on – a verse-type idea and a chorus-type idea. In dramatic terms this is helpful for a character who keeps swinging between two different ideas in their heads or a dramatic scenario with two dimensions to it. Traditionally, the choruses stay the same, even lyrically, although perhaps with small changes. This implies that one of those two ideas is a lynchpin – something that keeps drawing the character back, or something that needs to keep being repeated, or something that unifies everybody again having found divergence in the verses. The optional bridge section in a verse-chorus form can have the same kinds of functions as the B section in AABA forms; similarly a pre-chorus might provide an additional structural section that can help to draw the dynamic curve a little differently and provide a starker contrast between the verse and chorus if required. The potential for a more complex or 'busier' dynamic curve within a song shape can be seen with the various forms of the verse-chorus structure.

Matilda's 'I am song' from *Matilda*, 'Naughty', is a classic verse-chorus structure:

A – verse 1
A – verse 2
B – chorus
A – verse 3
B – chorus
C – bridge section which builds
B – chorus
D – short coda to round off the song

Matilda's message conveyed in her choruses in this song are her statement of her view on life and their repetition gives the audience a clear sense of her character, her determination and her strong sense of justice and willingness to stand up to authority when things aren't right. Matilda's verse sections are of a storytelling nature, and the bridge allows for her to take a slightly different tack and to build through the section through to a final resounding chorus, creating a sense of shaping and build. The dynamic curve for the song overall, as might often be the case for a song of this structure, would involve a relatively low level of intensification for the storytelling of the verse, rising for the chorus, then releasing intensification again for the next verse, and another rising back to the same chorus level as before. These alternations between intensification levels for the verses and the chorus are more like 'steps' than gradual curves – it is as if there is a step change for each of the sections. The bridge then involves a dip down which does then allow for a steady build of intensification through the bridge section, creating more of a gradual climb than seen previously in the song, before ending on a highpoint with the final chorus and coda which remains at a similar level of intensification to the final chorus.

A modified form of the structure can be seen in 'Misunderstood' from *Adrian Mole* which uses verse-chorus form to chart the journey of Adrian, Nigel and Pandora over the course of a Friday night. The chorus that is repeated takes on a different meaning of the characters being misunderstood as the dramatic journey unfolds. In the first chorus, it is largely a solo in which Nigel says he is misunderstood by his parents in terms of the fashions of the time and what he is allowed to wear. The second chorus is a communal sentiment of the teenagers feeling misunderstood in their pubescent journey. In the third chorus Adrian expresses how Pandora is misunderstanding his being found with the magazine 'Big and Bouncy', and in the final chorus it returns to the teenage universal cry of being misunderstood in the process of growing up. This song is a good example of how a repeating chorus section can be used to progress drama; they do not need to imply that repetition means that something has stayed the same – recontextualization is a really important tool, in which the same section of song takes on different meanings. The full structure of this song is:

Verse 1 (A) – Nigel solo regarding what to wear and getting ready

Pre-chorus – Mum's reaction

Chorus 1 (B) – Nigel feeling misunderstood by his parents

Verse 2 (A) – each of the teenagers getting ready – it becomes a shared experience with each in their own heads

Pre-chorus – company

Chorus 2 (B) – all of the teenagers feeling misunderstood

Dialogue underscoring – Nigel and Adrian

Bridge (C) – the first bridge is used for Adrian to express how he doesn't feel like he can fit in or win Pandora. This sets him apart from the other teenagers. He then restores determination.

Chorus 3 (B) – repetition of the teenagers feeling misunderstood

Dialogue underscoring – Adrian and Pandora, and Adrian and Nigel both asking Pandora to dance

Dance break – musical dance arrangement based on the chorus material

Verse 4 (A) – Pandora finds the magazine and turns on Adrian

Bridge (C) – Adrian tries to explain to Pandora that Nigel has stitched him up

Bridge 2 (D) – teacher confronts Adrian

Chorus 4 (B) – communal teenage expression of being misunderstood.

It can be seen that the complexifying of the standard verse-chorus form, with additional bridges and underscoring for dialogue aids the dramatic journey of the plot twists and turns that happen in the musical sequence, but it is all based on verse-chorus form, with each of the kinds of song sections (verse, chorus, bridge) having their own kind of function in terms of plot revelation.

Through-composed forms

Songs that are through-composed do not lean on the familiar song structures; they do not provide the familiarity of the repeated sections that are characteristic of all the song structures that we have looked at. Instead, they are truly governed by the mantra 'content dictates form' and they evolve musically as the drama evolves. 'Hysteria' from *The Light in the Piazza* is an example of such a song, which we looked at in Chapter 6 regarding its changing modes of enunciation. As we saw then, the music continues to change as the drama develops:

A – Clara speaks over a chugging instrumentation

A' – she sings a dotted figure over the chugging instrumentation, followed by a lyrical bar at the end of the phrase

A' – this is repeated with the next stage of her journey

B – she extends the previous phrase into new material as she starts thinking about waiting for Fabrizio

A" – the chugging figure is repeated but this time with increased dissonance, before she meets her first instance of feeling threatened

C – new material underscores her panic, characterized by vibes and pizzicato in the orchestration

A''' – another derivation of the chugging figure, with dissonant obligato oboe as Clara sings a short section of her A' melody to 'la'

C' – this seamlessly moves back into the vibes and pizzicato kind of material which wanders harmonically

D – a dissonant triplet descending figure begins in the orchestra to indicate her descent into further panic

E – Clara sees the museum that she recognizes and recalls the melodic theme from 'Passegiata' that accompanied the last time she was there with Fabrizio, however with increased dissonance

F – the dissonance heightens into chaos as Clara reaches the peak of her panic. This is similar to the D section, but moved on such that it is no longer a derivation of this – the musical language is the same but there are no longer the distinctive triplet descents

A'''' – Margaret finds Clara, and sings a short derivation of the original A melodic material, but in a different arrangement to any of the previous four versions of this thematic material. The music becomes still, peaceful and calm

G – a pre-reprise of 'Fable' to calm Clara further.

Each of these labelled sections is very short – they are more like the length of a phrase or two than the usual 'verse' or 'chorus' kind of length. The music is ever-evolving on a micro level, as each small moment of narrative unfolds. It can be seen that much as the song is through-composed, repetition is still used as a tool, and the song finds its grounding in thematic development, both internal thematic development of the original A material set out at the beginning, and also in invoking repetition of themes heard in the musical – one with associations with Fabrizio (E – 'Passegiata'), and the other with connotations of Clara's child-like relationship with her mother (G – 'Fable' pre-reprise). From a dramaturgical perspective, the composer in this kind of scenario has a palette of tools of material and is then literally following the dramaturgy moment by moment, sculpting the song as appropriate depending upon the dramatic circumstance and emotion.

Scene into song

As we have seen in principle with regard to big shapes, the shape of a song not only stands alone, but also changes the larger dynamic curve shape of the scene that it sits within. The scene without the song would provide a different portion of the larger dynamic curve of the show than it does with a song as part of its expression. We have already talked about this in regard to big shapes, but the point I would like to raise here is to do with the use of the dynamic curve to help the transition between scene and song. In the traditional book musical, it is often said that the transitions of moving between performance modes are moments that creatives tend to be very careful about because these can cause clunky gear changes; they are often the moments people who dislike musicals are wary of – the fact that characters suddenly burst into song. The transition into song can be helped by exploring its moment of joining and what that does to the dynamic curve on a small scale in that moment. Is there what is often called a 'ramp up' into the song, where the curve might be on a smooth incline upwards? If so, how 'steep' do you want this ramp to be? Should there be quite a fast trajectory into the song or do you want it to feel like it is gradually emerging?

The interface between dialogue and song in 'For Forever' in *Dear Evan Hansen* is an example of a smooth ramp. This is brought about through both accompanimental and vocal techniques. The opening of the song is naturalistic vocally in terms of the melodic rhythm following speech patterns and having a restricted range, close to Evan's speaking register. The entire first verse has held chords in the accompaniment, initially placed in the piano, and then guitar is introduced, also holding the chords per harmony change. This allows for a *colla voce* style – literally meaning 'with the voice' in Italian – where the band are following the vocalist. This allows for the performer to be as naturalistic as possible in their transition from speech into song, and also allows for some freedom of rhythm in their vocal line, again allowing for as naturalistic a presentation as possible. There is no riff, pulse or beat in the instrumentation – the vocalist does the leading. Not only does this ease the progression from dialogue into song, and is an oft-used technique for doing so, but in this particular dramaturgical scenario it also allows Evan the freedom to be slightly searching for the next bit of his story that he is fabricating throughout the song, rather than locking him immediately into a pulse which demonstrates more certainty. On arrival at the chorus, the piano begins a quaver figuration pattern which sets a pulse and a sense of riff. The vocals are also more stylized in terms of the use of a more expressive vocal melody. The shape of the vocal line in the chorus can be seen as a very distinctive climb and release with a small turnaround on the end of the phrase. The song is now locked into a pulse, the vocal melody is more expressive and the transition into song-proper is complete, albeit still light in texture and register at this point. Once the second verse introduction begins, the drum beat and bass also kick in and the song takes on its own groove and continues to grow and develop through the remaining song as Evan gets into his stride with the manufactured story of his day with Connor.

Or perhaps there isn't a smooth incline, and it is dramatically appropriate for song to burst into the scene or erupt in a sudden outpouring of passion. 'Paciencia Y Fe' from *In the Heights* is an example of this. The beginning of this song erupts into the scene as Abuela Claudia declares how hot it is through a single-word statement repeated at different pitches, with the orchestration delivering punctuated sustained chords, each one accented with the re-statement of the exclamation. The song's intensity lowers into the verse as Claudia reminisces and tells the story of past times in her life, but the opening of the song is at a high level of intensity, a sudden burst of energetic outcry. It can be seen that the transition from scene into song at this point would be a sudden jump up in the dynamic curve, almost like an interruption or sudden outburst of energy, functioning quite differently dramatically to the very gradual incline seen in the *Dear Evan Hansen* example. Using the dynamic curve will help these junctures to be navigated so that they have the desired narrative effect.

Musical phrases

Let's drill down even further for the final use of the dynamic curve that we are going to discuss, and look at musical phrase shape. It may be useful at this point to recall the discussion of Laban efforts from Chapter 3 where we discussed that certain characteristics of either personage or drama can influence the quality of the music parameters that are our composing building blocks. The dynamic curve is likely to refer most to melody in this way, and can be a helpful way of looking at the degree of expression that a certain character's melodic theme has. We discussed in the earlier chapter about range and tessitura, and how far a particular theme's melody might jump in terms of intervals, or whether it might be dramatically appropriate for it to have a more constricted intervallic range. The dynamic curve is another tool to add to your arsenal in this regard. There is a more direct correlation here as well in terms of conceptualizing the shape of the curve according to how far the melody moves on the piano keyboard, on the notated stave or on the region of your sequencing software.

The ideas we have discussed in relation to flat-line shapes which would be brought about by a restricted interval range, and more intricate dynamic curves brought about by a wider range in tessitura and intervallic leaps, all apply here but on a very small scale. In this way you can deliberately and consciously choose the extent to which your character's theme expresses itself on a small scale, and have deliberate control over each parameter of your score, making very conscious dramaturgical choices.

'The Party Goes with You' from *35MM* demonstrates a good example of shaping phrase by phrase in the vocal melody. We could label the first four phrases of the song as A, which are then repeated before coming to a chorus. If we split this A into its four component phrases, we can see the part that phrase structure plays in the shaping of the phrases, and the whole A unit. The characteristic shape that is being used is a step-by-step climb, pitch by pitch up to a peak and then a fall or return back down from the top of that peak. The first phrase could almost be seen as a complete basic dynamic curve in itself; slowly climbing up bit by bit to a peak and then tailing off, but only part way; not all the way back to where it started. If you compare this with the diagram of the basic dynamic curve on p. 76 you can see the similarity. The step-by-step shaping of this climb gives the impression of slowly drawing out the melody, bit by bit, giving a sense of sinuous movement. There are no sudden movements in terms of pitch jump or interval shape, and no angular movements; the smoothness of the pitch contour gives a sense of wistfulness, appropriate for the quasi-sensual quality of the character's memory. This first phrase climbs to a peak and then descends with a little tail. The second phrase starts at the same pitch as the first and has the same step-by-step climb, before being varied by having a longer tail on the end. The third phrase reaches the peak of this four-phrase unit, by completing the same step-by-step climb, before moving a little higher for the peak of the curve before descending. This is the mini climax of the shape of this whole unit. The fourth and final phrase mirrors a similar climb and descent, but with a smaller range, not having returned to the starting note of the other three phrases. It can be seen how each of these four phrases is its own dynamic curve, sharing shaping with each other so that they share characteristics, but the small differences between them in themselves create a larger-scale shaping of the whole unit, enabling this to peak at the third phrase before descending in intensity for the fourth phrase. The first phrase climbs, peaks and ebbs. The second phrase extends this by having a longer and more intricate tail. The third phrase develops this again by climbing higher than either of the other two. The fourth phrase lowers this peak by having a smaller range and a less extended climb and retraction than any of the others. This is small-scale shaping on a phrase-by-phrase basis. This first A section of 'The Party Goes with You' is a classic example of how a verse-structure can achieve both unity and development within itself, providing a satisfying shape: in this case the A unit is itself a basic dynamic curve shape, made up of four small dynamic curve shapes. Much like nesting dolls, dynamic curve shapes sit within larger dynamic curve shapes: a song dynamic curve is made up of various phrase dynamic curves; an act dynamic curve is made up of various song and scene dynamic curves and so on.

When the chorus is reached in 'The Party Goes with You', a different shape is created and this, importantly, distinguishes the chorus from the verse. While the dynamic curve shapes of the phrases in the verse were gradually growing and retracting, the chorus begins with a wide leap of interval and remains around what was the highest part of the verse dynamic curve shapes for much of the chorus. In this instance, as is often the case, the chorus is of a higher level of intensification than the verses. The curve shape for the chorus would consist of a sudden jump up – a very steep climb shape – and then maintain that high region for a few notes before descending. The second part of that first phrase then happens twice, a small curve upwards before a steep jump down. Then we have a repetition of the jump of the first phrase, with a similar descent, and then finally a third reiteration of that initial jump to the high region before a final descent. If you sketch this shape out roughly, and compare it with the verse, you can see the difference in shaping between the verse and chorus. The chorus does not gradually reveal lines; rather, the character has a more determined, less wistful, sense of confidence in these statements.

Summing up

We've seen that the concept of shape can be a highly useful tool when considering the collaborative ways that the performance disciplines interrelate with each other in the musical. It is helpful to the analyst to get inside how a moment might be working, and it is helpful to the creator to be able to use sketched shapes as a writing tool. The process can range from detailed considerations of modes of enunciation as compared against performance modes, and charting against emotional feeling to get a sense of where on the intensification scale each moment might be. Or it can be as simple as a sketched shape on the back of an envelope or on a large piece of A3 paper in the rehearsal room and used in a more intuitive way. The tools are there; the way that you want to use them, set the parameters and make the decisions is up to you.

9

Mapping the musical

In Part One we have looked at a variety of theoretical concepts and how they can be used as a shared language when approaching the score of a musical. These are intended to be your tools, your arsenal, your palette that helps to move from the blank page to populating your score in a symbiotic way with the development of the narrative of your musical.

We have looked at theory; we are now going to move into practice. You may be reading from the perspective of a composer on a creative team writing a musical; you might be a deviser who is part of a team that are devising a musical together or you might be coming from a more analytical standpoint: you might be directing a musical and finding ways to get inside it, or you might be a student needing to write an essay that includes analysing music in the musical. For each of you, the way that you apply the theory and tools that we have discussed will differ. Also, and most crucially, there is, of course, no *one* way to write or analyse a musical. The theory we have looked at can be applied in myriad ways, and it may be that just one idea or concept from our arsenal speaks to you and is applicable to your particular situation. The freedom, of course, is entirely yours to use the tools in whatever way suits you as a person and your creative circumstance. I am, however, going to apply the theme-shape tools in a sustained way in order to move beyond theory, help explain them in practice and suggest a way that they could be used in relation to the musical. We will explore this from two perspectives: that of the analyst (director, researcher, essay-writer) who is aiming to use the tools to dig deeper into the workings of a pre-existing musical and that of the creator (composer, deviser, theatre-maker) who is trying to generate new work. The next chapter will be for the analyst and will entail a case-study musical, systematically applying elements of the theory we have looked at in order to do a sustained analysis of the show. The final part of the book following that will be for creators, offering exercises and questions to help navigate through the process of creating a musical.

Before we leap into that, I would like to share one more analogy and that is the concept of mapping the musical. It can be helpful to approach the musical in layers, which is something that will be explored further in practice in the chapters to follow. To help approach that way of thinking, the concept of a map or a variety of maps that gradually zoom in to more and more detail of the geography of a landscape gives a visual idea of the process. If you are a visual person, the literal sketching of the musical at these different layers on multiple pieces of large paper can really help to establish and work out the theme-shape details of the piece. It doesn't have to be neat, to scale or follow any form of rule – it's your map and simply a part of your process in helping to refine layers of detail within that process. So here below are four types of map that can help with the analogy of layers; working through them sequentially will result in a gradual drilling down into the musical in more and more detail.

The overview map

First is the overview map. In geography, an overview map is a generalized view of a geographic area, like a zoomed-out bird's-eye view. In analytical terms this is called the 'high level': high-level analysis looks for patterns and meaning from the perspective of an overview of the whole, so in our case encompassing the whole musical and looking at the patterns from that perspective. The tools we have been exploring that will be included in the overview map are:

- The way in (see Chapter 1): here we consider the core of the show and therefore of the score, and how that infuses everything that is to come in the creation or analysis of the show. This includes decisions about style, about the fundamental techniques that might be used in the score regarding any musical rules or parameters, hand in hand with the dramatic rationale for these choices.

- Story and plot (see Chapter 2): the difference and similarities between these two aspects of the narrative that is being told, and how the choices made here impact the structuring of the show to come. A strong knowledge of the story being told behind the narrative will be needed to create an awareness of how that story is being told through the plot, and what role the score of the show has to play in that telling.

- The universal theme (see Chapter 2): at this overview stage there needs to be strong identification of the universal theme – the crux of the show thematically – which will also instruct everything that is to follow. The universal theme may give further influence to the composer as to the style and core of the fundamental parameters of the score.

The overview map is about getting the foundational building blocks in place: the absolute fundamentals of the identity of the show and the influence this has on the early decisions that are made about the core of the nature of the music and how it functions in this particular musical.

The base map

In geography, a base map is an outline map which gives basic information over which further detailed maps can be layered. This is similar to the way we use the term 'base' in clothing: a base layer over which other layers can be built. The base map for a musical would be like looking at the basic outline, the blueprint, the foundation that gives the context and impression of what can then be fleshed out with further detail. The base map involves drilling down a little further into the nuts and bolts of the musical than did the overview map. The tools and ideas that we will use for this second layer are:

- Identifying the key moments of narrative using the Lévi-Strauss method in order to reveal the trunk themes of the narrative (see Chapter 4).

- This then leads on to consideration of the relationship between the trunk themes and the score: for example, this might include consideration of whether there is a particular song that is aligned with a trunk theme, conveying clear musical thematic material in relation to that trunk theme (see Chapter 4).

- The dynamic curve shaping of the whole show, considering the 'big shapes' that are made in the show (see Chapter 5). This may include consideration of the dynamic curve brought about by the intensification levels of plot alone, and the dynamic curve as is created by all of the performance modes, addressing the question of how the score (and other creative aspects and performance modes) shapes the dynamic curve of the overall show at the high level. This will include identification of the highpoints and an awareness of how these are brought about, including what kind of highpoint they are.

- Consideration of modes of enunciation and how they function in the score in context (see Chapter 6). Inherent in this is the consideration of the dramaturgical rationale for certain modes of enunciation being used at any one time, as well as the consideration of the elements of music that will bring about the impression of this mode of enunciation.

- Consideration of extroversive semiosis – any references to the outside world in musical style or association – and further consideration of semiotic signs that are created within the world of the show (see Chapter 2). At this stage it is useful to be aware of how the associations that are made between certain musical materials in the show with particular narrative or dramatic elements can be used, adapted and carried through the score of the musical.

The base map really starts to get into the nuts and bolts of the show and helps to map out precisely which songs go where, with full awareness of the function that they are playing in that moment, both in terms of dynamic shaping in the show and in terms of any thematic and semiotic association. The base map really begins to feel like the show is mapped out in a workable way. The next layers are therefore about working on the detail of each of those moments individually.

The ordinance survey map

An ordinance survey (OS) map, the friend of keen walkers and ramblers, shows small detail relating to pathways and the different kinds of strands of paths, roads and byways. In our use of the OS map as an analogy, this relates to the smaller-scale detail of how the various strands might run through the course of the musical. Despite this kind of detail, an OS map can still zoom out to cover larger areas of a region. In this layer we start to look at songs individually and focusing on the crafting of each song, and the dramaturgical reasons for those crafting choices. The tools which we focus on in the OS map are:

- Song structures, looking at why certain structures might be used for either dramaturgical or stylistic reasons (see Chapter 8). Here, it can be considered whether pre-existing, traditional song structures are used song by song, or whether there is a more free, through-composed approach to each moment.

- Songs might be explored in strands: this might be approached according to the trunk themes as specific strands (see Chapter 4), or it might be that it is more appropriate to group songs by character, considering all of the musical material of a particular character in comparison with each other.

- It is at this point that Laban efforts are useful, when approaching the musical elements and characteristics of either certain characters or trunk themes (see Chapter 3). Laban efforts might be used to help consistency of character, or to compare and contrast characteristics between characters and how they interrelate with each other.

- Consideration of musical elements is important at this stage as appropriate: asking questions regarding the specific approach to melodic writing, to harmony, rhythm and orchestration for storytelling purposes in each moment (see Chapter 3).

The OS map facilitates song-by-song composition or analysis. It can be very helpful at this level to group songs according to either character or theme so that an awareness of each strand that runs through the musical can be maximized, rather than taking each song by song chronologically. The chronology is, of course, important, but belongs more in the higher-level viewpoint of the base map to see how the shape of the songs sits in their linear ordering. The OS map enables more dissection of the network between related songs and the way that the music creates and sustains these relations and character or thematic traits.

The street map

A street map gives the small scale very precise detail of a smaller-scale area, dealing with a particular town or quarter of a town. This is the map that you need if you are trying to walk from one specific building or street to another, and we shall therefore use it as the analogy of the smallest-scale level of detail in the musical: considering small units such as phrases and cells. The tools which we will employ in the street map are:

- How phrase shapes are constructed in terms of suitability for character – this takes the work being done in the OS map and continues it on an even smaller-scale level, considering how a character shapes their vocal lines on a phrase or cellular level.

- The spinning of musical material through the show and how this functions. This might include such techniques as:
  - Different types of repetition of small cells of material
  - Techniques of variation and derivation of cells to create related, or answering phrases
  - Considering the relationship between vertical aspects of music and horizontal, thinking about the way harmony and melody might work or interrelate for example.

- Consideration of branch themes and how they relate to the trunk themes of the show (see Chapter 8). This includes questioning whether there are small cells of musical material from the trunk themes that might become recontextualized and developed into something else to create a branch theme relation, *if* indeed this is the way that the score works for this particular musical.

- Identification of the palette of musical material on the small-scale cellular level, whether that be through the use of trunk and branch themes as indicated above, or whether it functions as a shared palette of cellular musical material. This is the small-scale equivalent of having an overview of the song functions which was undertaken in the base map: here we look at the network of small shapes and individual musical motifs which might be working throughout the musical.

The street map drills down to the smallest-scale level of the literal dots on the page: their small-scale shaping and their thematic relevance. At this point questions are considered about why each specific moment of music might be the way it is in the score for the show.

Summing up

This thought experiment of the four types of maps helps to solidify the idea of building a picture of the musical in layers. We can see how it is possible to take a systematic approach – if that is so desired – and build either an analysis, or indeed a score, layer by layer, each time drilling down to further depth of consideration about what is going on in the relationship between the musical material and the dramaturgy of the piece. And so, with this in mind, we will move on to the example modelling of how the theme-shape tools might be used in a systematic way in analysis in the next chapter, followed by a series of exercises and questions for the creators of musicals.

Part Two

Piecing it together
in analysis

10

Analysis of Everybody's Talking About Jamie

This chapter is for anybody who is analysing an existing musical, whether that is for scholarly reasons, or as a creative getting inside the show and its score more fully. In this chapter we will undertake a sustained analysis of the musical *Everybody's Talking About Jamie* (hereafter referred to as *Jamie*) with music by Dan Gillespie Sells and book and lyrics by Tom MacRae, based on an idea by Jonathan Butterell. The analysis will provide example of how the tools we have explored in Part One might be pieced together to give methods for analysing the score of a musical, analysing the score from the perspective of drama. *Jamie* was originally a stage musical which originally opened at the Sheffield Crucible before transferring to the West End. In 2021, a film of the musical was released, and it is this film version that I will mostly be referring to during the analysis in order to allow for ease of access for the reader. The film does contain some significant changes in songs (e.g. omitting Margaret's song 'If I Met Myself Again' and replacing 'The Legend of Loco Chanelle' with 'This Was Me') which undoubtedly changes the shape of the show; something which is an inevitable part of the transfer of a musical from stage to screen. It is the shape of the 2021 film version of the score that will be focused on here.

Usually, the analyst approaches a piece of work with a research question in mind. For the performer this may well be about getting to know the character as much as possible and therefore approaching the score with the intention of discovering what the music reveals about the character, in addition to the information given by words in the musical. For the researcher, there might be any number of varied questions being addressed in research, but I hope that the tools found here will be adaptable to the given circumstances. As it is unlikely that the researcher will simply be trying to find out things about the score in generalities, without a specific focus, I will aim to avoid a generalized analysis in this chapter. However, I should like to choose an angle which gives a wide enough scope to be relatable for the reader's own take. I shall therefore approach the analysis with the following research question at its heart:

What does the score of Everybody's Talking About Jamie *reveal about the development of the character of Jamie through the show, and his changing relationships?*

We will approach the analysis using the various levels of maps discussed in Chapter 9. While you would not necessarily structure an essay or piece of research in this way, in this wider-scope version of the analysis it will help provide a systematic framework, starting at the overview, high-level analysis and gradually exploring down through the layers to the smaller-scale levels, as outlined in the previous chapter.

The overview map

At the high level of the overview map we look at the nature of the essence of the score of the show and consider what some of the ways in may have been for the composer. When dealing with a musical from the canon, we can never purport to know what the writers were intending or thinking when they wrote the show, unless they have directly said so in interview. We cannot know the composer's methods of composing, and I am not meaning to suggest that they used the techniques discussed in this book. However, we are able to use some of these tools to closely explore the score in detail to see what might be there for the audience to receive and interpret. As with all analysis, it is about informed and carefully calibrated interpretation; each analyst will have their own interpretations and their own versions of the conclusions that they draw. As we have seen in all contexts in this book: there is no one way. We also consider the story and the plot, and what they begin to imply about the large-scale shaping of the show.

Jamie was premiered in 2017 and the essence of the score is reflective of its time: it has a contemporary score, creating a direct connection to the audience. The show is based on a true story, inspired by the 2011 documentary *Jamie: Drag Queen at 16* and the 'now' of the sound of the score creates a direct relationship between the audience and the characters on stage – they inhabit the same kind of soundworld that our contemporary life does, and the score therefore highlights the 'real-ness' of the story of the show. Jamie is a real person, and his music represents that reality. The show revolves around Jamie's dream of being a drag performer, and the influence of the soundworld of drag acts can be heard at the core of the score. There are certain moments in the show where songs are diegetic – that is the characters are literally, knowingly singing within their reality – in the context of drag performance and those songs sound in keeping as a unified whole with the entirety of the score, including the non-diegetic songs (the songs that are not literal performance in the characters' world). At first glance, there is no big shift in the soundworld between Jamie's life at school and his burgeoning life on the drag scene, perhaps suggesting the unification for Jamie of his personas; the show represents the coming together of his worlds and their unity within the person that he is. This is a score in which, I would suggest, the hook that holds the score together is one of style. The contemporary soundworld, inspired by the drag scene, is the style that gives birth to the score as a whole and creates for the audience the world of Jamie New.

Dan Gillespie Sells is a pop artist and writer, and the lead vocalist for pop band The Feeling which formed in 2005. The pop soundworld of the score for *Jamie* is informed by Gillespie Sells's style from many years of writing pop music. He has spoken in an interview about the importance of hooks in the score for *Jamie*. He speaks of the opportunity that it provided to write a score which 'lets everyone in', that doesn't 'put up any barriers'. Gillespie Sells speaks inspiringly about this trait of good pop music, that it is accessible and inclusive by letting everyone in. He says: 'A hook is more than just a catchy bit; it is simple enough for people to understand, and when they understand it, it lets them in' (Jamie.musical 2021). Not only is this inspiring for a musical theatre score in general, but it gives insight into the metaphorical sense of inclusivity and accessibility behind the score of *Jamie* which is the ideal vehicle for a show about a story which moves from prejudice to inclusion. It also informs us that the hooks are an important part of the score of the musical, and that they need attention to be paid to them.

As we have said, *Jamie* is based on a real-life story, that of Jamie Campbell, a 16-year-old from County Durham who has grown up with dreams of being a Drag Queen and who wins his fight to attend his school prom in a dress, supported by his mum, Margaret. This is the inspiration for the show, and the story of the life of Jamie Campbell is one story's trajectory which informs the story of the musical. However, as with all adaptation, this real-life story is the inspiration to the musical rather than the details of the story being adhered to. When we speak of the story of the musical, it is not this real-life story we are referring to, but rather the implied story brought about by the events of the plot in *Jamie*. The story and the plot of the show are closely aligned in shape: *Jamie* is a traditional book musical in its structure, and it has a linear narrative. The ordering of events in the plot has the same trajectory as the ordering of events in the story. However, there are some things that happen in the story which we are not witness to in the plot, for example, in the plot we never see Jamie rehearsing for his set at Legs Eleven, but that he has been practising is implied. We do not witness the exams that Pritti, and all of the classmates including Jamie, are taking, or the work for them, but the fact they have done them is implied by their reaching their leaving prom. However, in terms of a rough shape, the plot tracks the trajectory of the story of the show and so this is not an instance where the ordering of events in the plot has a significant impact on the interpretation of the story.

The universal theme of the show is about identity. Jamie's journey charts through his exploration of identity. Initially the drive of this is in the discovery, creation and reveal of his drag queen, Mimi Me, before moving into further exploration of his identity as Jamie New. In relation to our focus question about the development of Jamie as a character, and his relationships, the nucleus of that is the development of Jamie's self-awareness and relationship with himself – with himself as Mimi Me and with himself as Jamie New – and how each of those identities interacts with the world around him.

The elements of the overview map establish *Jamie* as an identity, coming-of-age musical in which everything radiates out from the protagonist's exploration of his identity and what that means in terms of his relationships with those closest to him and with the world around him, including those that encourage him and those that block or taunt him. The traditional book musical structure of the show and linear narrative indicates that the story is told in a linear fashion and that dialogue and music play equal roles in the storytelling. Dan Gillespie Sells points to this symbiotic relationship between the script and score in interview: 'The script and the songs are like two entities that co-exist and as soon as you change one element of one of them the other one has to change to adapt to it' (Jamie.musical 2021).

The score's contemporary pop soundworld aids the theme of inclusivity in the show, enabling access to the audience, letting them in through its hooky score. The contemporary soundworld aids the reality and the immediacy of the original source inspiration and roots the show in the contemporary world.

The base map

In the base map of the show we look at the overall dynamic curve shape of the musical and the intensification of moments in this regard. Consideration of the highpoints is key to this, as is identifying the most 'stress-full' parts of the narrative, as discussed in Chapter 2 in relation to the Lévi-Strauss method, which will reveal the trunk themes for the show. Let's begin here, identifying the key moments of intensification narratively:

Margaret gives Jamie his first set of heels for his birthday.		
Pritti encourages Jamie to go to Prom in drag.		
	Dean bullies Jamie and Pritti.	

Jamie goes to the House of Loco for his first dress.		
	Miss Hedge humiliates Jamie in school by demanding he go to class with his faulty make-up.	
Jamie performs as Mimi Me at Legs Eleven.		
Jamie goes to school in make-up.		
	Miss Hedge forbids Jamie's make-up and his plans to go to prom in a dress.	
	Pritti urges Jamie to be himself at Prom.	
		Jamie reveals his body loathing as himself.
	Pritti tells Jamie that in Arabic his name, Jamil, means beautiful.	
	Jamie is rejected by his father.	
		Jamie is angry at Margaret and rips his dress.
		Jamie becomes destructive.

		Hugo encourages and comforts him.	
		Jamie and Margaret make up.	
		Jamie arrives at prom as himself, in a dress.	
	Miss Hedge tries to refuse Jamie entry to prom.		
		Jamie's classmates rally and fight to allow him entry.	
		Jamie and Dean make amends.	

The process of splitting the narrative into its key moments and placing them in this format, inspired by Lévi-Strauss, such that horizontally the events give the timeline of the show, and vertically it gives thematic groupings, reveals four trunk themes. The left column shows the positive moments leading to Jamie's creation of his drag queen Mimi Me; the second column demonstrates prejudice and rejection towards Jamie in various forms; the third column reveals all the elements of support towards Jamie and acceptance of himself as he is; and the fourth reveals moments of Jamie's turmoil and desperate upset. These columns can be seen to reveal some key themes which stand counter to each other: Mimi Me standing in relation to Jamie New; the theme of rejection versus acceptance. These will become the four trunk themes for the analysis:

- The identity of Mimi Me
- The identity of Jamie New
- Rejection
- Acceptance

In this way, and in relation to our research focus question, it can be seen that at its base map level, the show is in fact entirely about Jamie's development as a character and his relationships. Of fundamental importance to that is the question of Jamie's relationship with himself, both as Jamie New and as Mimi Me and how those relationships develop over the course of the musical.

Let's look at the dynamic shaping of the musical from the perspective of how Jamie is feeling about himself and his identity at any one time throughout the course of the musical. We can see from the chart above that broadly speaking the first half of the show focuses on the trunk theme of Mimi Me and her identity, whereas the second half of the show focuses on the identity of Jamie as Jamie New, and how he feels about himself at any one time. This inevitably gives a dynamic curve shape to the musical which is in two halves; interestingly each half being of a broadly similar shape to each other, each involving a climb throughout the half, with some dips along the way.

The show begins with Jamie expressing a sense of hope and optimism about his future, although he is knocked by classmates, particularly Dean Paxton. This narrative beginning is at exposition level of intensification on the dynamic curve, with Jamie's sense of self-worth rising up the dynamic curve with Margaret's gift of red sparkling shoes, and then rising further with Pritti's encouragement for Jamie to wear them to Prom. Despite feeling nervous, and unsure, Jamie eventually finds further encouragement in the House of Loco and determination to create his drag queen identity; another rise in the dynamic curve. The moment along this trajectory that knocks Jamie's feelings of self-worth is Miss Hedge's insistence that he walk through the school wearing his make-up that has gone wrong, in order for Jamie to be ridiculed. However, Jamie reclaims this moment and turns it into an empowering event, quoting Hugo's words that drag queens are to be feared, thereby climbing further up the intensification levels of the dynamic curve in relation to his feelings of self-worth. There are further insecurities as Jamie prepares for his set at Legs Eleven, but with Hugo and the other drag queens' encouragement, he continues to climb the intensification curve with the highpoint of this trajectory being his performance as Mimi Me at the club, and his classmates' explosion of attention in response to this. The peak of Jamie's feelings of self-worth following this climb of the dynamic curve throughout the first half of the musical is demonstrated by his going into school in make-up. We can see that broadly speaking, the dynamic curve shape in relation to Jamie's feelings of self-worth is one steady climb, albeit with undulations of doubt along the way, with the root of this confidence of identity being in his growth of identity as Mimi Me. At the highpoint, Jamie's strength of relationship with Mimi Me is at its strongest level of empowerment.

Miss Hedge's rejection of Jamie at this point, along with Dean Paxton's bullying, causes Jamie's feelings of self-worth to plummet, and so taking the dynamic curve back down to a low level. This can be seen as the start of a new journey for Jamie. Having reached the highpoint of confidence in his identity as Mimi Me, Jamie starts a new journey of learning to feel confident as Jamie New. Pritti's encouragement causes a rise in dynamic curve but the lowest point of confidence comes with Wayne's crushing rejection of Jamie leading to Jamie's period of self-destructive behaviour. Again, it is through the encouragement of other key characters (Hugo, Margaret) that Jamie's feelings of self-worth takes another, steeper climb of dynamic curve leading to the second highpoint in the show of Jamie's acceptance of himself as Jamie New, demonstrated through going to Prom as himself in a dress, along with garnering the acceptance of Miss Hedge and the rest of the school. Essentially the show has two halves: each characterized by a climb to a highpoint.

So, what role does the score play in these dynamic curves?

Songs in *Jamie* occur at key moments of identity portrayal, with each song being about revelation of identity in some way. They have less of a function of conveying plot; rather, the score aligns itself with a primary purpose of creating heightening regarding each moment of realization of identity. 'Don't Even Know It' creates a heightening of identity for Jamie in his mind beyond what his classmates know of him; it elevates the moment way beyond the boredom of the class situation they are in, creating a steep raising of the dynamic curve in that moment. 'Wall In My Head' relates to Jamie's early discoveries in relation to his identity and the wounds inflicted on him about this by his father, Wayne. 'Spotlight' encourages Jamie to present a new identity in drag, again projecting a much more heightened moment than the scenario that Pritti and Jamie are in in their classroom. 'This Was Me' diverts the attention to Hugo, but still very much being about identity – his identity in the past – and making Jamie aware of how this relates to his own identity. 'Work of Art' forces Jamie to become public with his drag identity and is an important heightening moment in which the wider school becomes aware of his intentions for drag and about his forthcoming performance. 'Over the Top' launches Jamie's new identity as Mimi Me and 'Everybody's Talking About Jamie' is the fallout of this in which everybody gets to know of the identity of the new Jamie. 'It Means Beautiful' speaks of a truth of inner identity and a peaceful acceptance of that. 'He's My Boy' turns the sense of identity to a relational one, and a sense of loving possessiveness on the part of Margaret. In 'My Man, Your Boy' Jamie affirms this relational identity, acting as a partner song to the one previous. Finally, 'Out of the Darkness' is about identity within community, moving into identity acceptance and celebration. As we can see, each song of the score of *Jamie* is a part of the universal theme, truly rooting the score in pursuit of exploration of this theme.

The first half of the show is where the songs are at their highest level of upbeat pop drive. For the most part they are in dance mode, with an intention for rhythmic drive. This can be seen in 'Don't Even Know It', 'Spotlight', 'Work of Art' and 'Everybody's Talking About Jamie'. It can be seen to a lesser extent in 'Wall In My Head' which could arguably be said to start in song mode, but ultimately the song also has a strong sense of rhythmic drive to it. All of the songs in relation to Jamie in the first half of the musical are in dance mode – there is a strong propulsion of energy to the score. 'This Was Me' has the feel of a song in dance mode, although the dramatic circumstances and story that it is telling lean into song mode in terms of its intention to affect. It is partly through extroversive reference that such an affect is created: the 1980's soundworld, which is used for 'This Was Me', places the storytelling strongly in the time period of the 1980s and thereby links the time period with the associations of the story of the AIDS crisis that is being told. In conjunction with the footage being shown of Loco Chanelle in the 1980s, and placing that fully in reality with footage of Princess Diana visiting patients with AIDS, the extroversive reference makes a powerful statement about the time period in the real world and drawing it in to the world of Jamie and Hugo in this contemporary moment. The dance mode of the 1980's soundworld is evocative and affecting because of its context with the story that Hugo is telling and our associations with the reality that that was. This soundworld is not heard again in the show, and is reserved as a particular heightening device completely tailored to this moment of Hugo's back story. The contrast with the song from the stage show that it replaces – 'The Legend of Loco Chanelle' – is interesting. The stage song is also in dance mode but without the aspect of song mode and affect that the film song has. 'Loco Chanelle' is also in keeping with the style of the rest of the show and so that contrast provided by the 1980's extroversive reference is not there in the original. Arguably 'This Was Me' alters the dynamic curve shaping more than 'Loco Chanelle' because of its contrast stylistically and its allusion to song mode within the first half of a musical which is largely devoid of song mode.

'Over the Top' is the song which launches Jamie onto the stage as Mimi Me, with her lip-sync performance embedded within the original song. This song plays on extroversive references in two ways: first it plays on dotted rhythms which seem to both complement the militaristic imagery in the lyrics and give a nod towards a tango-type rhythm indicating an association with passion and a fire in the gut. Both of these references are helpful in terms of relating to what Jamie is doing regarding the bravery of his journey, launching Mimi Me in front of jeering classmates at the club. 'Over the Top' also contains a section of Mimi Me's performance lip-synching to Beverley Knight's 'Kiss the Sun'. This source music song from the real world gives an additional dimension of semiosis in terms of using a song that is known to the audience within the context of an original song for the show. Other source music is used in the film as a backdrop to sequences such as Jamie's working for his new dress, but this is the only moment where an existing song is diegetically incorporated into the musical, making this moment stand out amidst the score. This launching of Mimi Me is the start of the first highpoint region of the show, starting here and continuing through the title song, 'Everybody's Talking About Jamie', through to Jamie's entrance to school in make-up. The use of source music at this moment allows for this difference in the soundworld, and highlights it as an important moment due to the contrast with the rest of the score, and thereby the highpoint is ignited. It is interesting that Jamie does not sing as Mimi Me non-diegetically, but she only 'sings' in the context of this lip-sync performance, adding to the sense of this being a marked, significant moment. This highpoint of the show in the creation of Mimi Me and Jamie's feelings of confidence also marks the end of the story's focus on Mimi Me; this moment is both a highpoint and a conclusion. This is the moment that the whole of the first half has been working towards, and its highpoint is reached musically through this combination of source music and the distinctive militaristic references, again, unheard anywhere else in the score.

The high region is continued through 'Everybody's Talking About Jamie' through the use of high energy; this is arguably the most driving and most high-energy song in the score, creating a high level of intensification through sheer pace. This pace is especially necessary to create the sustained high region because the majority of the songs of the first half have been in dance mode and have already had quite high levels of energy. Indeed, several of the earlier songs – 'Don't Even Know It', 'Spotlight' and 'Work of Art' – invoke imaginary glamorous scenarios of performance, catwalk and stardom (these are particularly played upon visually as well as musically in the film version with the fantasy sequences created, in contrast with the stage version which keeps these sequences in Jamie's reality). The songs in these moments raise the dynamic curve further than the level that the book is at in those moments, creating higher intensification of spectacle both musically and visually. So, when the moment of performance and stardom arrives for Jamie in his reality then the additional pace and breathlessness of the excitement of his classmates are necessary to lift the dynamic curve even further than those earlier moments of spectacle have done musically.

The second half functions differently in terms of how the score shapes the dynamic curve. The songs which follow the first highpoint are largely in song mode. As we have seen, it is in this half of the musical that Jamie develops in his relationship with himself as Jamie New, as opposed to his relationship with himself as Mimi Me; this is less about show stardom and more about the internal work necessary to accept himself and to heal the scars, left by his father Wayne in particular. These are introduced in the song 'Wall In My Head' early in the show, but it is in this later part of the show that these ideas are developed further. It is Pritti Pasha whose song transports the score to song mode in 'It Means Beautiful'. Because of the deletion of 'If I Met Myself Back Then', Pritti's song is the first ballad in the film version of the musical, and it marks the lowering of intensification in the score following Jamie's altercation with Miss Hedge. The orchestration is markedly different from everything that has been heard so far, starting with intimate solo acoustic guitar, only growing in texture to include string ensemble. There is no rhythm section to the song; no drumkit and no electric bass. It is essentially a film-version of an unplugged, acoustic song, stripping back all of the drive and electric-powered band that has characterized the score thus far. This intimacy is powerful, musically metaphorically stripping away Jamie's layers for Pritti to strike at his heart and its beauty. Jamie has just confided in her that he feels ugly without Mimi Me and Pritti's response of beauty is in the simplest textural form found in the show. Its simplicity makes it stand out, and makes it beautiful, operating in song mode with the intention to affect through its simplicity. This song does not create an intensification of dynamic curve through any significant heightening; instead, it is highly significant in its acoustic simplicity to begin the journey of affecting and of Jamie finding true expression as himself, not just as Mimi Me.

'He's My Boy' and 'My Man, Your Boy' are both bigger texturally, and both return to the plugged-in soundworld and use of rhythm section, but they are both still ballads, expressing strong emotions and with the intention to affect in song mode; both songs speaking of the powerful relationship between Jamie and Margaret. Because of the omission of 'Ugly in this Ugly World' and the reprise of 'And You Don't Even Know It', these three songs in song mode follow one from another in the film version, creating a large region of the score in song mode, each song highlighting a key relationship in Jamie's life and in his steps to acceptance of himself. One of the key differences to the deletion of 'Ugly in this Ugly World' is that Jamie's sequence of self-destruction in which he shoplifts, drinks and appears on the football stadium in front of his father happens during Margaret's song 'He's My Boy'. The juxtaposition of the song with the heartbreaking visuals of this sequence heightens its nature to affect even more. In his devastation, Jamie is not given singing voice in the film version. Song is not used as a means by which Jamie rages or expresses the depths of his grief about his relationship with his father, or his feelings of self-worth and identity. It is for Jamie's mother and best friend (Pritti) to carry the score through this section, metaphorically holding and supporting him until he is able to express himself again vocally in his apology to Margaret in 'My Man, Your Boy'. When dance mode returns in 'Out of the Darkness' at the end of the show, it is as if the journey of extended song mode has now influenced dance mode, with a calmer sense of serenity to the uplifting finale.

The songs in *Jamie* change the dynamic curve in the first half of the show in as much as to continually raise it higher than it would be otherwise, always elevating and pushing the boundaries, metaphorically representing Jamie's similar pushing of boundaries and reaching for elevated modes of expression. In the later part of the show this reverses, and the songs shape by affect, growing in emotional truth rather than performative elevation.

Summing up

The base map has revealed key, fundamental features about *Jamie*:

- We can identify four trunk themes, brought about through application of the Lévi-Strauss method of looking at the narrative: Identity as Mimi Me; Identity as Jamie New; Rejection; Acceptance

- The dynamic curve of the show at a high level seems to produce two halves with an overarching growth to a highpoint in terms of Jamie's self-worth which is important in our understanding of our focus on Jamie's development and relationships (other factors could be placed as the focus of the dynamic curve giving different results)

- There are two highpoints in the musical: one as regards the launching of identity as Mimi Me, and the second as regards acceptance of identity as Jamie New

- The songs function as indicators of the theme of identity, each exploring this in a different way

- There is a prevalence of dance mode for a significant amount of the show, with an extended period of song mode occurring in the second half of the musical indicating Jamie's period of doubt and grief.

OS map

We now fill in more detail in our mapping of the musical, turning to focus on the level of the OS map. At this level we will look at individual songs in more detail, looking at what consideration of Laban efforts in relation to the score might reveal about character dynamics. We will also look at the song forms that are used and what they contribute from a dramaturgical perspective.

It is interesting that the voice of rejection and oppression in *Jamie* is not given singing voice. Neither Dean Paxton nor Wayne has their own songs, or express their lack of support for Jamie in song. It is this fact that is likely to play an important part in the positivity of the message of inclusivity in the show; to deny a character singing voice is a powerful statement in the arsenal of a composer and to not musicalize the voices of hatred leads to an ultimately hope-filled score, which is important for the universal theme of exploration of identity in our times. The stage version allows Jamie to wrestle with his own self-rejection in song in 'Ugly in This Ugly World' but the film even removes that from its musical language. The one moment of oppression delivered through song is Miss Hedge's attempt to humiliate Jamie in the song 'Work of Art', but this presents a different scenario than would have been the case with a song from either Dean or Wayne, because of Jamie's act of turning the moment around to one of active positivity and declaration of his identity, rejecting Miss Hedge's attempt for humiliation. With the exception of the first part of 'Work of Art', it is therefore Jamie's *supporters* who are given score time and musical voice. Between the trunk themes of rejection and acceptance, it is only the stages of working towards *acceptance* that get airtime in the score of the musical. The characters of Pritti, Margaret and Hugo and the drag queens are therefore the people whose characters are developed through the score of the musical, alongside the principal character himself.

Jamie's songs

Let's begin with the songs that Jamie sings about himself; the songs that Jamie originates: 'And You Don't Even Know It', 'Wall In My Head' and 'Out of the Darkness'. Jamie's vocal lines in 'Don't Even Know It' have a tendency towards the 'dab' effort. After the first few phrases, his vocal lines are direct, often involving only one or two notes. In the pre-chorus section, the vocal line often simulates a fast reciting around an E, before alternating between the dominant and tonic – the B to the E. The chorus also often revolves around a melody that is constructed from alternating between two notes – C# and E. While this is a predominantly quaver rhythm, rather than the earlier semiquavers, the effect is still one of dabbing, lightly touching one note to the next at a fairly fast pace. The dab effort gives a sense of liveliness to Jamie; a lightness of touch, a sense of pace and a character with surety of mind – an impression that is brought about through the directness of the vocal line melody, working in conjunction with the confidence of character portrayed in the lyrics. In the orchestration, the opening light synth bounces with a dabbing effort right from the start, with the bass riff, drums and finger clicks all confirming the dab effort.

However, there is a secondary effort in the song which is a more sustained one. The piano and strings are sustained in the verses, over which Jamie's vocals dab, and in verse 2 this is taken to the level of a tremolando in the backing – a smooth, gliding backing for Jamie's vocals. The sustained glide effort gives a smoothness and a coolness over which Jamie can operate. Jamie's verses vocally are also of a more sustained effort. These phrases do not last for long before hitting the dabbing of the lengthy pre-chorus section, but they indicate more of a float effort: they are more indirect in terms of shape, and have slightly more of a sustain as they fall down each phrase.

Halfway through the choruses, Jamie's vocal line is taken higher into a falsetto range. This contributes to his lightness of vocal touch, but not in an ethereal way as we saw earlier in the book in relation to Orpheus in *Hadestown*. Because of the context of the funk style of the song, the falsetto here places Jamie more in the realm of a star vocalist operating over the top of the backing singers in a rock context, rather than a lightness of ethereal otherness. Indeed, Jamie is structurally placed even more as the frontperson of a band in the film version of the song than even in the stage version. The cut that is made for the film version deletes the rap section in the middle which gives more introduction to Jamie's classmates and to Miss Hedge. Instead, given the fantasy stardom sequence of the visuals of the film version, which places the song outside of the literal context of the classroom in a fantasy world in Jamie's head, the protagonist is very much placed as the sole subject of the song and its focus; the others are there as backing entourage rather than being introduced in their own right. The Laban efforts of 'Don't Even Know It' place

Jamie upfront and centre with confidence and directness, but with a lightness and coolness of touch.

'Wall In My Head' is the only song in the film that Jamie sings privately. It is an internal moment as compared with all the other outward-facing songs. In fact, the only other internal song in the film at all is Margaret's 'My Boy'; all the others have a sense of shared community about them. With the deletion of 'Ugly in This Ugly World' in the film version, 'Wall In My Head' does a lot of work in terms of revealing Jamie's inner insecurities. Being the next song after 'Don't Even Know It', the internal nature of it contrasts with the showmanship of the first number; it is here that the truth of Jamie's vulnerability is revealed. The effort of Jamie's vocals is still direct and light here, but there is a smoothness to them, with more sustain which suggests a glide effort. This is certainly the effort established in the introduction through the piano and strings sustained chords. However, this song also shows Jamie's determination to keep moving forward, and the effort is changed via a performance choice part-way through the song. With the change from lightness to a more heavy sound, the effort is changed to press rather than glide. This dramatically makes sense in terms of imagery as Jamie fights back at the wound that is being recalled and continues to press forwards to overcome it.

'Out of the Darkness' is the final song, in which Jamie reaches resolution and acceptance. If Jamie's first song has been about his projected stardom, brought about through mostly dabbing efforts, and 'Wall In My Head' is about Jamie's insecurities and determination, portrayed through gliding/pressing efforts, 'Out of the Darkness' combines these two featured efforts. As we shall see in the street map section below, there are some familiar contours of vocal shapes used in this song, which bring together the themes and characteristics of the show into this sense of resolution. And so is the case in terms of efforts: Jamie's vocals both dab (primarily in the pre-chorus) and also glide (in the early verse and in the chorus) in turn. This sense of energy and precision alongside a gentle sustain seems to be representative of the character of Jamie that we get to know during the show. The section that feels new in terms of vocal contours is that of the bridge where Jamie sings a vocal melody that spans a wide range. Starting on a top A in falsetto range, he moves down in stages, first by step and then to the C#, before starting the second phrase in sequence, singing the same shape but transposed so that in total the whole phrase has covered a span of a 9th. Jamie's vocal lines have largely not covered such a wide range in a short space of time before and this kind of range seems to have been reserved for the moment where he is able to declare his conclusion and call to arms to everybody, including the audience, to find their own voice. Another factor which makes this section stand out significantly is that it is the only one of Jamie's three core songs that has a bridge; and this *is* that bridge section. All three songs share a very similar song structuring: verse-chorus songs which include pre-choruses to build into each chorus and a coda at the end with an extended riffing on the themes of the song (more about this in the street map below). The verse-chorus structures are typical of the pop style of the show, but they also give the maximum potential for the 'hooky' feeling that Dan Gillespie Sells speaks about in the interview mentioned previously. Gillespie Sells speaks of how important the hooks are in terms of relatability and there are hooks in these songs, not only in the choruses, but also in the pre-choruses in particular. Dramatically, they imply a central thought or message to the song that keeps being returned to in the chorus. This is certainly the case in Jamie's songs: in 'Don't Even Know It' that message is about his future stardom, in 'Wall In My Head' it is the return to the idea of the battle that he has to do within himself after the hurts created by his father and in 'Out of the Darkness' the returning message is one of belonging and new beginnings. The songs are not focused on or structured around Jamie going on journeys of discovery within them; rather, the song structures allow clear, bold statements of purpose. Each one has a dynamic curve shape of gradual build and in this way show a song-shape that is similar to the shape we have discovered at the base map level that happens twice in the show: the overarching gradual build to a highpoint. Jamie's songs mostly continue to grow throughout them: in the case of 'Don't Even Know It' growing to the end, whereas in 'Wall In My Head' and 'Out of the Darkness' Jamie has a small tail at the end of the large extended coda.

Jamie's songs establish a primary repertoire of three efforts: dabbing, and gliding which moves into pressing with more variation in heaviness. This mixture of quick and sustained efforts infuses the majority of the score, constructed, as we have established, from characters' voices who have a positive impact on Jamie and his development. This fusion can be seen in

'Work of Art' which is the one song in the film version that contains negativity towards Jamie, which Jamie reclaims and turns into a positive statement for himself. This song clearly contains both the efforts of the sustain of gliding and the quickness of dabbing in quite pronounced ways. Structurally the song is an alternation of verse and chorus, with one specifically used pre-chorus in which the classmates use the already-implemented technique of fast, dabbed, spoken rhythmic repeated lines at Jamie. Generally speaking, the verses (both sung by Miss Hedge) make use of glide effort, with a smooth, light-voiced sustain which is exaggerated by the deliberate emphasized vocal slides at the ends of phrases. The string lines also slide in a way not otherwise heard in the score, producing string effects that create an almost nightmarish, out-of-body or internalized experience for Jamie, being on the receiving end. This internalized soundworld effect is enhanced by the muted electronic-sounding kick drum, playing a four-to-the-floor pattern which is more akin to the 'punch' effort, contributing to the sense of attack on Jamie. The chorus makes use of the dabbing effort, also in a semi-exaggerated way, with short, snappy phrases involving alternation between two notes, which are reminiscent in a marked way of some of Jamie's earlier melodies. It is after the pre-chorus that the soundworld opens up into more of the pop-style orchestration heard in Jamie's songs, and he confidently takes over the chorus. The alternating melodic pattern here is clearly in the world of Jamie's vocals – the nightmarish sliding and muted internalized sound thrown off – and 'Work of Art' becomes an addition to Jamie's outward statements regarding his identity.

Let's move on to Jamie's relationships with those closest to him by looking at the songs of his best friend, Pritti Pasha, and his mum, Margaret, followed by an exploration of the songs of the drag queens who support him along the way.

Pritti's songs

Pritti plays an important part in encouraging Jamie through her songs, first in 'Spotlight' and then in 'It Means Beautiful'. In 'Spotlight' she encourages Jamie to wear his new heels to Prom and to step out into the limelight, and in 'It Means beautiful' she encourages him to know that he has inner beauty just as himself. Through these two songs, Pritti is instrumental in speaking to both sides of Jamie's exploration of identity. The effort conveyed through the vocal lines in both of Pritti's songs can be seen as 'float'. In both songs, Pritti's vocal lines covey a wider range per phrase shape than a lot of Jamie's phrases do. The way that her vocal lines work in pairs of short phrases (as discussed below) means that part of the shape's journey is traversed in the first part of the phrase, and the rest of it in the second, meaning that she has travelled quite a lot in range, but only in stages. This sense of travel can be argued as being indirect (as opposed to wide intervallic leaps for example which might be considered direct). Her vocals have a lightness of touch, just like Jamie's, and there is a sense of sustain written into her vocals. This is brought about by two techniques which are seen less in Jamie's vocals, both of which draw the vocal rhythms across the beat. The first is the use of triplet rhythms as seen in the verses of 'Spotlight'; these give a sense of drawing out the vocal line bit by bit in a sustained manner working over the beat. The second is the use of back-phrased rhythms, seen a little in 'Spotlight' but much more so in 'It Means Beautiful'. For example, the rhythms on the word 'beautiful' each work across the beat, delaying the final syllable by a quaver and displacing other movement to the off-beat, such as the words 'grey' and 'kiss'. This rhythmic technique, coupled with the balladic style of the song, gives a drawn-out sense so that there is a smoothness of sustain rather than a rigidity of rhythm to the grid of the down beats. Both the triplet rhythms and the syncopated ones give a feel of back-phrase; of stretching out the vocal line, which becomes a feature of Pritti's songs and indicates a thoughtfulness of character. Just as seen in Jamie's songs, both those sung by Pritti are verse-chorus structured songs. However, they are both a simplified version of the verse-chorus structure as opposed to those seen in Jamie's songs, both of them using only sections of verse and sections of chorus; there are no pre-choruses, bridges or codas. The dynamic shaping of these two songs is also different to those sung by Jamie. 'Spotlight' demonstrates a classic dynamic curve shaping, growing to the second chorus, mostly brought about through a thickening of orchestration and backing vocal texture and dynamic growth, before gently receding and lowering the dynamic curve of intensity at the end. 'It Means Beautiful' has a fairly flat dynamic curve shape in terms of overall growth, but it is on the level of smaller-scale phrase shaping that undulation is brought about and the song is given shape (more on this below in the street map). In this instance, the more gentle shaping of that song gives a sense of calm and stillness, appropriate for the moment in question. Pritti's character speaks of truth in its many senses, and the simplicity of her song forms and dynamic shaping all speak to this portrayal of a rock-solid, determined and gentle beauty of truth.

Margaret's songs

Jamie's relationship with his mother Margaret, as discussed, in the film version of the score is portrayed through the songs 'He's My Boy' and 'My Man, Your Boy'. 'He's My Boy' contains several musical features which make it stand out in the context of the rest of the score: first it is the only song that is sung without Jamie's presence. 'Everybody's Talking About Jamie' also insinuates that he is not there for a large part of it, but the visuals of Jamie's arrival at school in glamourous style indicate that he is aware on some meta level of what is being said about him in the song. 'He's My Boy', however, has a feel of separation about it. Margaret sings of the unbreakable love she has for her son, and set in contrast with the surrounding scene in which he walks out on her, that absence brings about a sense of grief – an absence that is not depicted anywhere else in the show. Second, it is the only song in a time signature that is not 4/4. 'He's My Boy' is a 6/8 ballad – the only section of the show in a compound time signature – again, giving it a different feel to the rest of the show and highlighting its significance. Third, vocal range in this song spans a very wide, two-octave range from low F3 to top F5. This indicates a large build for her in the song, which is indeed what happens structurally: the dynamic curve of the song is a growth towards the highpoint of the end of the bridge through to the final chorus, and then a stripping back and swift descent of the dynamic curve for the tail at the ending. Fourth, this is one of the very few songs in the show to contain a bridge section and a modulation brought about through that. The growth in intensification in Margaret's song is arguably one of the largest in the show. It starts minimally, with a simple, repeated, piano triad, beginning the song in Bb major. The chorus section starts with a G minor harmony, but remaining in the Bb context and cadencing to Bb at the end of the chorus. The bridge takes the song into a tertiary-related move harmonically, modulating to Gb and moving through a sequence that means the return of the chorus is a tone higher than the song started in, and the song ends in C. This kind of heightening brought about by modulation of tonality does not appear very much in the score to *Jamie*, and therefore makes this a highlighted moment musically. In addition to this being an important song because of the vital nature of the relationship between Jamie and Margaret, it is also, in the film version, the container for the expression of Jamie's grief, as well as his mum's. As we have seen previously, it is during this song that we seen Jamie go off the rails because of his own feelings of devastation. But because these are not given voice directly from Jamie in the film, it is as if Margaret is giving voice to those feelings as well as her own. Margaret has a lack of directness to her vocal lines, involving vocal riffs and undulation of phrasing, and her phrases indicate a sense of sustain. As with Pritti's vocal lines, this is not achieved through long sustained notes but through a certain kind of shaping that involves drawing out each phrase smoothly. At the beginning of the song, the music is indicated in the score to be piano (quiet) in dynamic, with indications of accents, crescendoing to forte (loud) and fortissimo (very loud) at the interface between the bridge and the chorus: the growth of dynamic and vocal strength is specified within the score. As such, the vocal quality at the beginning of the song is light and becomes increasingly heavy throughout the song. Margaret therefore begins the song with a floating effort, and gradually moves through to 'wring': sustained, indirect and heavy. This is the only occurrence of the wring effort that we have seen in the score, and it is an appropriate effort for the expression of intense emotion, such as is found in this song.

'My Man, Your Boy' is the next song in the film musical's score after 'He's My Boy', and this is also significant in its portrayal of the relationship between Jamie and Margaret. It is the only song in the show which is, in itself, relational because the second half of it functions as a duet. In the rest of the score for *Jamie* choral and backing vocal textures are used extensively. However, this song is different, in that Margaret responds to Jamie's first two verses, pre-chorus and chorus with a polyphonic vocal line; an independent line to his and yet equal to it, interweaving with Jamie's chorus melody. This texture marks an important moment of coming together and a cementing of their relationship, just as the song more widely speaking represents a coming together of the relational aspect of Jamie's exploration of identity. The main part of the song is a solo for Jamie, but it is different to his other songs. He draws on the kind of melody lines of Pritti – stretched, drawn-out lines that have a more indirect use of trajectory than his previous song. Lyrically he is drawing on Pritti's message of beauty at the start of the song, telling his mum that she is beautiful; passing down the line the encouragement of seeing beauty in oneself that originated with Pritti in 'It Means Beautiful'. The song also draws on fragments heard in the preceding song 'He's My Boy' (explored further in the street map) while drawing on the same lyric imagery of the 'man' versus 'boy' in relation to his mum. This song is a coming together of ideas through this region of song mode that result in a coming together of Jamie's sense of inner identity and in relation to others and those closest; bringing together musical features which have been heard from both his best friend and his mum. 'My Man, Your Boy' has a truncated sense of structure: it consists of two verses, then a pre-chorus and then two choruses. This somehow fits with the sense of summing up and pulling ideas together in that rather than develop musical ideas of its own, it is drawing together ideas from previous imagery and thereby seems to function more like a rounding off and completion of 'He's My Boy'.

The drag queens' songs

Beyond his best friend and mum, the other support for Jamie is from Hugo (aka Loco Chanelle) and the other drag queens at Legs Eleven. The two songs which form this strand in the film version are 'This Was Me' and 'Over the Top'. We have already discussed the stylistic importance of these two songs; it is through style that this thematic strand is given distinction – not through any consistent style for the drag queens, but by the fact that each of them stands out from the overarching contemporary pop style of the rest of the show. Orchestration plays a large factor in their distinction, with the use of 1980's drumbeats, synths and risers in 'This Was Me' and in the use of trumpet fanfare-style solo obligato lines in 'Over the Top', alongside the militaristic dotted rhythms and drumming. Jamie does not sing with the drag queens, but rather they are both songs in which a baton is metaphorically passed to Jamie. 'This Was Me' is one of only three songs in the show to have a bridge section, indicating a change of thought or circumstance, with a longer structure of song to give more scope for traversing a journey of storytelling in the song. The other two as we have seen are 'He's My Boy' and 'Out of the Darkness' – one being a statement of grief and love, and the second being one of hope looking to the future. 'This Was Me' is both of those things: the song expresses the past grief of Hugo's love lost to AIDS, and also the hope of passing the baton to Jamie; something that Hugo literally does in the lyrics of the bridge. The orchestration in the song is used in such a way as to bring about changes in intensification in more of a marked way than we see elsewhere in the show. The opening verses start at a low level of intensification with a repeated harmonic piano riff, growing in texture in the pre-chorus where synth is more prominent, and growing again in the first chorus which adds a four-to-the-floor kick pattern and more synth string lines. This is stripped back again, lowering in intensification for the next verse, with a riser into the second chorus which opens out into a much fuller electronic orchestration. The intensification is stripped back again for the next verses, including one spoken verse, before a double-length riser gives even more of a boost of intensification in the third chorus than the first two. These contrasts between the much lower intensification of the verses and the ramp-up into the much-heightened choruses give a dynamic curve shape which portrays a sense of journey, of three sets of rising to a peak and lowering again. This sense of journey has a profound effect on Jamie, and is the factor that gives him the courage and determination to return to the shop and carry on the fight that Hugo has imparted to him.

'Over the Top' is similarly a song that is shaped by contrasts. The first entry of the drag queens, following Hugo/Loco Chanelle's solo militaristic verses, is a close-harmony sustained rendition, almost anthemic or hymn-like in its approach to block harmony, with minimal accompaniment. This is, again, a different texture to the majority of the songs heard in the show. The third verse returns to the solo militaristic nature, before an instrumental in which Mimi Me is introduced to the crowd. We have previously discussed the lip-sync section that occurs at this point, providing a strong sense of heightening musically and dramatically. Off the back of this heightening, in the return of the 'Over the Top' close-harmony chorus, the orchestration is much fuller and with the use of solo trumpet obligato lines over the top of the vocals, heightening the song even further so that the high region is maintained for the end of this sequence. The contrast between this version of the chorus and the almost a cappella texture of the first chorus helps to create this sense of soaring and launching of Mimi Me in the second half of the song, by drawing back in texture to then be able to pull out all the stops from that lower-intensity baseline.

Summing up

The OS map of the score of *Jamie* fleshes out the approach to the songs from the perspective of character and relationships. To summarize, some of the key points discovered are as follows:

- Every song in the show is sung either to or about Jamie; the score is entirely directed towards his character and journey
- Four strands can be seen to make up the score, each of which demonstrates the propulsion of the score towards helping Jamie in his journey of identity:
  - Songs Jamie sings and the way they indicate his journey through the show
  - Pritti's songs (the best friend's influence)
  - Margaret's songs (the mother's influence)
  - The drag queens' songs (the influence of the drag queen community)
- There is a prevalence in the score of 'dab' and 'float' or 'glide' efforts. This is not absolute, but rather points to an indication that the use of time (sudden or sustained) is played upon to give contrast and character indications. Pritti and Margaret's efforts are largely sustained, whereas Jamie's are often dabbed, with some elements of sustain, thereby pinpointing a certain amount of the energy of the score as arising from his character

- Only positive, supporting characters sing in the show, with the exception of Miss Hedge whose song ('Work of Art') is taken over by Jamie and also turned into something positive. Sung language is therefore only used to reinforce a positive message about Jamie rather than give voice to those that are critical

- The songs are often statements rather than dramatic journeys of discovery

- Jamie's songs become more relational towards the end of the show. This indicates the dramatic move away from his focusing on himself to his finding his acceptance of himself relationally and with the support of his community

- Every song in the show is a version of a verse-chorus structure. This is in keeping with the pop style of the score, and with the composer's feelings of importance concerning the use of hooky material. It also dramaturgically allows for statements to be made and returned to in the chorus sections of the songs – repetition is important at the level of the songs' structure. We will see in the street map that it is also an important feature at the level of the smaller phrase structuring

- Pre-choruses are an important feature, in Jamie's songs in particular. They allow for build and for ramps of intensification to be created

- Extended codas, similarly, are used in Jamie's songs in particular

- Three songs include longer structures which include bridge development sections; each one of them is important as a fuller exploration of an emotional topic. 'This Was Me' takes Jamie on Hugo's life's journey, involving a passing of the baton from mentor to mentee; 'He's My Boy' is an outpouring of both love and grief from Margaret but also on behalf of Jamie; and 'Out of the Darkness' allows Jamie to expand on his concluding life view at the end of the song

- Orchestration is an important part of the storytelling with some examples being:
  - The 1980's soundworld of 'This Was Me'
  - The internalized, nightmarish sounds of 'Work of Art'

- ○ The militaristic trumpet soloing of 'Over the Top'
- ○ The stripped-back acoustic simplicity of 'It Means Beautiful'
- ○ The use of builds, textures and drumming patterns to create contrasts in intensification within songs in order to raise and lower heightening and provide emotive shape.

Street map

Finally, we come to the street map, looking at the small-scale level of detail and how the spinning of material works in the show, both from the perspective of branch themes and from the perspective of how musical material is spun. In Part One of this book, we discussed the possibility that the narrative trunk themes of the show – and we have revealed four in *Jamie* – might have a central song each, from which branch themes may be developed and from which cells might be taken which become manipulated in a new context to form a new song which is tangentially related. There are perhaps a couple of very specific small moments of this in *Jamie*, such as in 'Your Man, My Boy' when Jamie specifically sings the same phrase shape on the word 'Mum' when the chorus lands as Margaret sang on the word 'boy' in 'He's My Boy', thereby cementing the relational aspect of that song and partnering the two songs about their relationship together. However, for the most part it feels more appropriate in *Jamie* to speak of a network of branch themes, without specific semiotic meaning, but that all intertwine with each other to build up the overall score and layers of meaning. We have already determined that every song in the show pertains to Jamie and his sense of identity in some way. We have then looked at the strands of the support surrounding Jamie in terms of his journey of identity, and how the songs can be seen as being grouped according to character to that end. This is slightly different from the idea of trunk themes which have related key songs, from which other branch themes can be spun. Instead, there is a palette of techniques in the score for *Jamie* which are utilized at different moments, creating cohesion between the songs, and contrast when required. We are therefore going to look at some of these techniques of construction in the score on a small-scale level, looking at small-scale shaping and spinning of material. First, we will look at some melodic techniques, and second, we will look at some harmonic elements. Many of these techniques are those that are particularly aligned with writing pop songs, as may be expected from this particular score whose pop style is at the core of its identity as a show.

Types of repetition

Repetition is a really important compositional device in *Jamie*. It is used in a variety of different ways. The simplest place to start is the prevalence of single note quasi-reciting that is used in the show. It is usually employed as a means of delivering impact: a fast-paced rhythmic repeated cell that creates energy and drive. In its purest sense this can be seen in the backing vocal to 'Out of the Darkness' where reciting on one note is heard for three cells in repetition before the fourth gives slight alteration to round off the full phrase. It is Jamie who begins the first version of this technique though, in 'Don't Even Know It' in the pre-chorus. After the first eight bars of verse, the pre-chorus involves a repeated phrase which in itself comprises repeated notes, initially reciting on E before dipping down to the flat 7 (D natural) before returning to the E and touching on the minor third above before returning to the tonic again. This phrase sets up important cells that are found elsewhere in the whole score: as well as the single-note reciting, the dipping down to the flat seventh of the scale and the alternation between two notes a minor third apart are both features that are carried through the show. In particular, the alternation between two notes is a key characteristic, found predominantly in Jamie's vocal lines. In 'Don't Even Know It' it becomes the main driving shape of the melody. It begins in the pre-chorus where the melody is a repeated cell of two dominant notes falling to the tonic – B to E. In the chorus, the repeating alternation becomes between the sixth note of the scale, C# and the E. In the second half of the chorus, the C#-E alternation is modified into diminution, now moving at a semiquaver pace rather than a quaver pace. The figure is displaced within the bar, starting with two C#s, then two Es, before there being just one of each pitch. In response to this, the cell that was Jamie's tune in the pre-chorus with the dip down to the flat seventh becomes a backing response from the company of classmates. The pre-chorus two-note alternation of two Bs falling to an E is taken up the octave in the second chorus for Jamie, placing him in falsetto range above the rest of the ensemble. On their fourth repetition, they are embellished by dropping to the fourth and the flat third as a kind of mordent (a form of grace note embellishment). This becomes derived further as a repeating response in the final chorus for the classmates, as they sing the title hook, broadly spanning from dominant to tonic, but this time more embellished, filling in the phrases at the third (G#) and offering an alternation there before falling to the tonic. We can see the cellular approach to the score clearly in 'Don't Even Know It' where there are three predominant cells that are repeated, varied and reconstructed in various ways. This leads to the extended coda where the cells come together in repetition, round and round in joyful celebratory exclamation. These cells are found elsewhere in the score. In 'Spotlight' the backing vocals move step by step to the minor third alternation on 'all eyes on me'; 'Out of the Darkness' makes use of the minor third alternation in the second part of the cell of the opening phrases; the verse of 'Everybody's Talking About Jamie' makes extensive use of the cell that dips down to the flat seventh. In 'Wall In My Head' the alternation of two notes is found extensively again, but this time the interval is a tone. The repetition of the word 'building' or 'climbing' in the song continues the persistent repetition of the alternation between the A and B. This is heard in retrograde on the repetition of the word 'head' which falls from the A to G, thereby pivoting the melody around the A in these moments and either climbing up away from it or falling down from it in a kind of loop. This loop imagery of the melodic construction is helpful dramaturgically in terms of the loop that Jamie feels trapped in in his head, expressed in the song as a wall over which he must continually climb. The repetition in this instance is almost like being on a treadmill, climbing up one step at a time but going nowhere, portraying Jamie's frustration.

The use of repetition can also be seen extensively as a technique for building longer phrase shapes or section structures in the songs. For example, in 'Everybody's Talking About Jamie' the opening five notes of the vocal melody create a short phrase, or cell. They are repeated exactly, before being sung a third time again, but this time extended into a longer cell. This whole phrase comprising the three short phrases is then repeated again, thereby creating a complete verse via two repeated lines, each one of which is made up of two repetitions of a cell and a third derivation of it. The repetition operates on both a cell level and a phrase level, and then the whole section is repeated (with different lyrics), thereby operating on that level as well. This is a common structuring device in the show (and in pop music). The verse of 'It Means Beautiful' involves the statement of a phrase (albeit longer than the first five-note cell of 'Everybody's Talking About Jamie') and then a repetition of that phrase, before a third phrase which is a derivation of the initial idea. This creates the verse structure which is then itself repeated. In 'Out of the Darkness' the first vocal phrase comprises a six-note cell that is repeated twice with a final tag of 'you're home' on the end of it. The second phrase of the verse that follows is then a repetition of the first. It is a technique that is used extensively, whereby verse or chorus structures consist of a repeated phrase which then has a closing derivation of it on the third or fourth iteration. It can be seen that this technique cements the 'hooky-ness' of the music, establishing a cell through repetition before becoming looser with it to finish the short section.

Repetition can also function alongside transposition: a cell or phrase is repeated but up a tone for example, or other intervallic difference. This is also seen extensively in the show. It is clearly evident in 'Everybody's Talking About Jamie' alongside strong senses of key change. We have already discussed the shaping and construction of the eight bars of the verse, which is then dramatically passed on to another group of classmates. This shift goes hand in hand with a key change to mark the sense of passing the rumour around. This is called a sequence, whereby a melody is repeated but transposed. In 'Everybody's Talking About Jamie' this sense of sequence is on a relatively large-scale basis; it is the entire verse shape which is repeated alongside modulation, shifting up a tone each time from E to F# to G# and so forth. However, this can occur on a smaller scale with sequence being the technique that is used to construct a phrase or section shape. In 'He's My Boy' it can be seen in the pre-chorus as the first melodic phrase about Jamie breaking Margaret's heart is then sung a tone lower; just for that moment the material is spun further in sequence before moving on to another shaping. This is picked up by Jamie in 'My Man Your Boy' where the first phrase of the chorus is repeated having moved down a tone, and then for the third phrase it begins the same with another tone's descent before then moving into a derivation of the phrase and becoming a different shape. A similar technique can be seen in the chorus to 'This Was Me' where phrases one and two create a sequence before phrase three starts the next bit of sequence but then takes the shape elsewhere. All three of these are descending sequences, in contrast to the rising sequence of 'Everybody's Talking About Jamie' which inspires a sense of rising heightening of intensification. The technique of sequences allows cohesion and the rooting of cells of material before then varying that same material into something else allowing the music to move on.

Phrase shaping

Continuing the idea of phrase shaping, we have looked at versions of repetition that help to create phrase shaping, but there are a couple of other techniques that are found throughout the score. One is to do with rising phrase shapes. There are two versions of this, both of which can be found in 'Wall In My Head'. First is the octave leap as a direct, targeted intervallic jump to create a sense of impetus into the next section (usually a chorus). In the second phrase of the chorus of this song, the intervallic leap is indeed an octave. At the beginning of the chorus, however, it is an ascending leap of a perfect fourth. This gives sufficient sense of jump to launch into the chorus, but the leap is extended to the octave for the repetition of the same lyric line in the second phrase. Both of these first two phrases of the chorus to 'Wall In My Head' create the phrase shape of a leap upwards which is followed by a descent back down, from which to leap up again and then fall back down again. This can be seen as appropriate dramatically for the context of imagery of trying to make it over a wall which keeps building and contributes to the sense of determined onward movement in the song. An octave leap is also used in 'Spotlight' at the same juncture between verse and chorus, where Pritti leaps from a B3 (just below middle C) to a B4 the octave above in order to catapult the melody onwards into the chorus. The octave leap gives a sense of gloriousness and an expansion of revelling in the music at this point. There is a similar technique used for Pritti in the transition between verse and chorus in 'It Means Beautiful', although in this instance the leap is the interval of a minor seventh rather than the full, perfect octave. Neither 'Spotlight' nor 'It Means Beautiful' have pre-chorus structures which help to create build between verse and chorus, and so the large intervallic leap is a means of creating that ramp within the bar that is the interface between verse and chorus. The second kind of rising phrase shape is literally brought about by phrases which climb in pitch bit by bit. It creates a questioning kind of inflection melodically, as raising the inflection of the voice on the end of a spoken question might do. This can be seen in the verses of 'Wall In My Head' as each short cell, repeated to make the fuller phrase, consists of a short scalic figure, continually giving a rising inflection. This leads into the two-note rising repeated figure already discussed and therefore this notion of constantly having short rising loops that repeat – as we have already seen – is maintained even further. The whole of 'Wall In My Head' seems to be constructed around shapes which rise in some way – be it rising phrase shapes, rising two-note figures or larger intervallic leaps – before either falling down to, or directly returning to, the original starting point. As discussed, the metaphorical imagery is clear. These kinds of shapes are also seen in 'Out of the Darkness' alongside the alternating figures characteristic of 'Don't Even Know It'; the rising inflection seems to be a characteristic of Jamie's vocal lines in particular.

Two-part larger phrase shaping is a particular feature of Pritti's songs, as alluded to in the OS map. In 'It Means Beautiful' the first two phrases of the verse are a repetition of each other, and in that way form a larger pair of phrases in themselves as the first four bars of the verse shape. This is then paired by a second four bars which is one longer answering phrase, taking the ideas of the contours of that first phrase but extending and developing them to round off the verse. We have seen similar examples of this kind of technique already, but seeing them as two halves to the verse structure gives a sense of call and response within the full shape. We said earlier that the overall dynamic curve of 'It Means Beautiful' is relatively flat, but that at the phrase level there is much more sense of undulation. The dynamic curve of the verse could be seen as a rise to a gentle peak and then a fall in the first phrase, followed by a second rise and fall in the repeated second half of that phrase. The second half of the verse then revolves around low A as a pivot note with a leap of a fifth before descending, followed by a leap of a sixth before descending again and then tailing the phrase off upwards by a step. This shape can be seen to have a gentle rise and fall, followed by a second rise and fall and slight curve upwards. The entire verse dynamic curve therefore consists of four rises and falls with a gentle tailing off upwards; we can see that the shaping of the phrases has a lot of gentle undulation compared with some of the recitation or two-note alternating shapes that make up much of Jamie's sung content. Shaping occurs more significantly on the small phrase scale rather than at the level of the song structure.

Two-part shaping in Jamie's songs tends to happen more at the section structuring level where his verses, pre-choruses or choruses might tend to have two themes within each of them. For example, returning to 'Don't Even Know It', the pre-chorus there has the recitation motif, and it has the dominant to tonic motif, as if the pre-chorus is itself in two sections. The chorus to 'Out of the Darkness' similarly has the title theme component to it, but also has the rising 'place where we belong' section to it, as if this is a second chorus theme. As we have discussed, in Jamie's songs, this variety of thematic hook material – all of which is contained within short cell-like phrases – allows for a mash-up of this palette of building block material in the extended codas. The other characters' songs tend not to function in this way, with longer phrase shaping instead, such as indicated in 'It Means Beautiful'.

A final thought on phrase shaping is the idea of broadly similar shapes being shared between characters when dramatically appropriate. Specifically, this can be seen in the influence of Margaret on Jamie when his phrase shaping in 'Your Man My Boy' is similar to that of 'He's My Boy'. Jamie sings in longer phrase shapes in this song than in his other material. The vocal shaping of the trajectory of the song is also related to Margaret's previous song in the sense of both starting the respective songs low in their vocal register and maintaining a sense of climb through the vocal range across the trajectory of the song. We see Jamie being influenced by other characters in certain lyrics: expressing his mum's beauty to her having been influenced by Pritti, as we discussed previously; the title phrase of 'Out of the Darkness' having originated from Pritti's lyric in 'Spotlight'; the use of man, boy and son imagery found in 'Over the Top' and in 'He's My Boy' before being used in 'Your Man My Boy'. These small details of musical phrase shaping demonstrate a degree of musical influence from the other characters on Jamie as well.

Harmonic characteristics

We have focused a lot on vocal melodic writing, but there are some characteristics found in harmonic techniques in the show which recur. We are perhaps less aware of them than the vocal techniques used, but they must also be acknowledged as part of the storytelling palette of the score.

The approach to the score is largely diatonic with functional harmony (this means that it uses chords which are expected within the key of the song). This is in keeping with the soundworld of this particular show; there are other soundworlds and contexts where the use of chromaticism plays an important role in the storytelling, but that is not a part of the toolkit for this particular show. An exception to this, within the bounds of functional harmony, is in 'Work of Art' where harmony does have a role to play in the nightmarish sense that we alluded to before. 'Work of Art' is built upon a chromatic repeating bass riff. This use of the word 'chromatic' does not mean in itself that the harmony is no longer diatonic – simply that the horizontal sense of the line uses notes outside of the scale that the song is in. Some of the string lines, however, do give a sense of chromatic harmony, alongside the string techniques such as tremolo and portamento that are used – the latter giving a top layer that has a sense of deconstructing the harmony of the song. 'Work of Art' is the only time this is found in the show and is specific to the dramatic moment in which Miss Hedge tries to humiliate Jamie in school.

The pre-chorus before Jamie's chorus in 'Work of Art' demonstrates a technique which is used elsewhere in the show; the harmonic pedal. This is a bass note – usually the tonic or the dominant – which remains constant for a period of time and over which the harmony shifts. In the kind of instance as in 'Work of Art' it creates a sense of building anticipation, heightening the dynamic curve in the ramp-up to the release of the chorus. However, it is used in other instances such as the verse of 'Don't Even Know It' (where the four-bar chord sequence is E – E7 – A/E – E) and the beginning of 'Spotlight' (where the first four bars of the verse is a repeated two-bar tonic pedal of B – E(add9)/B). In these contexts, the tonic pedal helps as a transition from scene into the song, letting the vocal establish before moving into full chord changes.

The descending bassline is another feature of the score; indeed, it is one of the characteristics that hold 'He's My Boy' and 'My Man Your Boy' in partnership with 'He's My Boy' having a descending bassline in the chorus and the latter song using the technique in the pre-chorus. A couple of final techniques include the translation of the flat seven – seen as a melodic feature in 'Don't Even Know It' and 'Spotlight' being used as a harmonic device in 'Spotlight' where the fall to the chord of A in the ninth bar following the tonic pedal constitutes a move to a chord on the flattened seventh. And finally, the highlighting of the possibility of repetition of harmonic progressions, just as much as the repetition of melodic cells discussed above. This repetition is seen in 'Wall In My Head' where the harmonic progression is the same in both verse and chorus, and indeed in the coda. The shaping of growth in the song is brought about through other musical means of melodic shaping, and orchestration and texture whereas the harmonic patterning of the song remains consistent throughout.

Summing up

The street map of *Jamie* demonstrates a variety of small-scale shaping techniques which are used as a palette throughout the entirety of the score. This provides cohesion and contrast, and is a method of composing which utilizes building blocks of musical material. Many of the techniques are shared between characters and theme but we have seen instances where there are specific techniques that seem to relate more predominantly to some characters than others. For example, Jamie is most likely to have melodies which revolve around alternated notes and recitation-like techniques, whereas both Pritti and Margaret have more undulating phrase shapes. This can also be seen to go hand in hand with the use of dance mode versus song mode which was referred to in the base map, with the recitation and alternating note patterns giving more rhythmic impetus for when dance mode is required.

The composer as dramatist

Having discussed the four levels of mapping of the score of *Jamie*, we return to the original focus question about what the score of the show reveals about the development of the character of Jamie and his changing relationships. We have seen that the score of Jamie is entirely about his character development, identity and the relationships in his life, and we have commented on the function that those songs all play as statements about the different facets of Jamie's sense of identity and relationships within the show. Looking at the songs in strands relating to characters in the OS map was more profitable than analysing them as regards the four trunk themes in the context of this particular show. This is because *of* those four trunk themes (Identity as Mimi Me – Identity as Jamie New – Acceptance – Rejection) we discovered that rejection is not given much voice in the score, but is more the domain of the book. Acceptance and the growth of the two sides of Jamie's identity are therefore the impetus of the entirety of the score, and all of the songs are either *about* or sung *to* Jamie in some way. By looking at the songs according to character strands it therefore helps to identify the characteristics of the different types of support and encouragement surrounding Jamie in the show. The two-part dynamic curve shape of the overall show, revealing a highpoint at each of Jamie's acceptances of identity, also helps to indicate the role that each song plays within those trajectories. Hugo and the drag queens help Jamie along the dynamic curve to the launching of Mimi Me; Pritti has a key part to play in both dynamic curves – one song for each; and Jamie's relationship with Margaret is fully given weight in the score in the latter stages of the show in relation to Jamie's acceptance of himself as Jamie New. We have seen that using the tools and concepts discussed in Part One of this book in a systematic way via the use of the different maps enables a gradual drilling down into the detail of the score, beginning with the overview, high-level analysis of musical function within the context of the storytelling and moving through the layers to the small-scale detail of compositional techniques. What remains is a strong conviction that the score of *Jamie* has his development of identity at its core and the range of techniques that can be seen in terms of how this is achieved within the pop-style identity of the score itself.

Part Three

Piecing it together in the creative process

11

Collaborative workbook

In Part Three, we come to the practical part of the book. What follows are a series of exercises, aimed at creatives. My hope is that you will be able to undertake these exercises collaboratively, whether that is just as a pair, or in a group of devising creatives who are creating a musical. It is possible to do the exercises as an individual as well, but much will be gained from the collaborative nature of doing them as a team. There are exercises that can involve everybody in the team, from designers to actors. As you might expect from the nature of this book, the exercises are geared towards helping to create the score of the musical, but there are times where I have indicated where the same exercise might be repeated with a different (e.g. choreographic/visual) focus in mind. There are exercises, particularly as we move into the realms of the street map, which are indicated as composing exercises. These are aimed specifically at the person, or people, who are creating the nuts and bolts of the score of the musical, be that through notation, through software, through improvisation or other devised performance means.

Each section starts with a list of the primary questions that are the focus of the exercises belonging to that area. If it is preferred, you could use these questions in checklist form as the basis for discussion or internal pondering, rather than working through all of the exercises.

The exercises are based on the four layers of maps that we have looked at in the last couple of chapters. They relate to all of the concepts discussed throughout Part One, but they are ordered according to the maps which get into more levels of detail as we move through them progressively. As you move through each of the four layers, I hope that you will get a sense of truly mapping out the musical and building it up with more and more flesh on the bones in more and more detail. Remember that the intended impetus at all times is to make every decision for a dramaturgical reason.

You will need lots of large paper – A3 size or a roll of lining paper – pens and sticky notes, and be prepared to be surrounded by lots of pieces of paper for a while.

So, let's begin.

Layer one: The overview map

The overview map helps us to get in to the show from out of the starting blocks. This is the foundational layer, where the initial building blocks are put into place.

Primary questions

- What is the universal theme for the show? What lies at the heart of everything?

- What is the way in for this score? What is the score's primary language, characteristic or hook that everything that follows can develop from?

- What would consideration of 'style', 'techniques' or 'leitmotif' contribute to the previous question? Is there a different aspect altogether that could be the way in for this particular score that derives from the concept of the show?

- What is the story that lies in the background behind this show?

- What is the plot – i.e. *how* do you want to tell that story?

- What is the function of song and music in the show? What purpose does it fulfil dramatically?

This show is …

This exercise aims to get to the heart of what your musical is about, its aesthetic, the way it feels and its key features.

With your collaborators, be that one other person, your creative team, or your devising group, take it in turns to finish the sentence 'This show is … ' adding something about the show.

Make a note of each of the items that come up from the exercise on a large piece of paper.

When you have finished, take four pieces of paper and give each a heading of 'Feel', 'Concept', 'Theme' or 'Other'. Assign the words that you originally came up with to one of these pieces of paper so that you have a grouped collection of words pertaining to each aspect of the nature of the show.

From your 'Themes' group, is one of these the universal theme? If not, repeat the exercise again until you are all in agreement about what you think the universal theme of the show is.

The mood board

Create a mood board for your musical. A mood board is a collection of images which all convey something of your musical: things which inspire, which give a feel and a flavour of the kind of world you are trying to create. Even though the composer's job is aural and not visual, it can help to have visual stimulus to feed into your process.

If you are working on a project with a designer, ask them for their mood board or for any sketches which might help to convey where they are coming from creatively with the piece. If it's more appropriate, make your own (even though this won't be 'official' for the project, it can still help your own process). This can be done either in a physical scrapbooking sense, or online using mood board tools, or simply collecting some pictures from an internet search.

Once you have some visual images in front of you that give an idea of what the show might feel like, start compiling a playlist of tracks that you feel somehow 'work' with the visuals in front of you. At this stage, they might be from a variety of sources without a sense of unity, but that's fine – you are just collecting ideas at the moment.

Once you have a playlist, which tracks are you particularly drawn to? Why is that? What are the features of those tracks, in terms of musical elements, that are noticeable characteristics of the piece? What compositional techniques, instruments, rhythmic elements or any other parameters or characteristics might you want to use for inspiration for your show? [Note, of course, you can't use actual samples or snippets of these tracks due to copyright – this is simply an exercise for inspiration rather than usage.]

After you have completed this exercise, is there anything that results helpfully regarding style or techniques, and what this might mean for your score in terms of core characteristics?

Leitmotifs

Spend a moment asking yourself if there were characters or themes that had leitmotifs in this show, who or what would they be. Sketch down your answers.

Does this make sense as a way in to your score? If you are having to think too hard about it then it probably doesn't make sense as the core of the music.

Composing exercise: Techniques

Are there any specific musical or mathematical techniques that might be at the core of your show? By way of example, it might be that the show involves a series of tannoy announcements and so the musical interval that often accompanies an announcement such as this (often a falling minor third) becomes an integral part of the score. Again, this is one where if there is nothing that makes sense to your show and you can't think of an example, then move on to the next exercise.

If there is – for example there is a sequence of numbers that are dramatically related to your musical – then spend some time sketching with this technique or sequence. How might it translate itself into music as a kind of cypher or dramatic code at the foundation of the score? Does this make sense dramaturgically as a hook that helps you get in to your score at all?

Composing exercise: Style

This is an exercise for when it does not seem obvious to you what the style of your musical might be. Let's consider style in relation to your musical with this brief exercise.

Write a four-bar melody inspired by your universal theme. For this exercise, it only needs to be something very quick and sketchy, and which is melody only.

Quickly make a list of four different styles that might be related to, or appropriate for, your musical in some way. I am not suggesting that each musical takes on the guise of the style of something else: these four different styles might relate to various elements of *your* composing style. For example, it might be that the show has a very lush romantic kind of a sound, or a more brittle hard-edged kind of world, whether it is set in the future, or the past.

Now try and either play, write or create in some way, an impression of how that melody would work in each of the four different styles, complete with harmony and accompanimental pattern.

Reflect on what each of these brings to the piece in terms of dramaturgy and try to make your decision from there.

Layer two: The base map

The base map involves lots of sketching and diagrams. This is where we will work out the overall shape of the whole show and the role that music (and other performance modes) play in that.

Primary questions

- What are the key moments of the narrative?

- What are the trunk themes of the show?

- How are the trunk themes represented musically? Is there a particular song that most encapsulates each of the trunk themes?

- What is the relative function of music as compared with dialogue and dance in the show (and any other performance languages that might be part of the specific piece – e.g. audiovisual aspects, or puppetry)?

- What parts of the show are best expressed through song? Are these moments of emotional intensity? Structural intensity? Both?

- What are the highpoints of the show – where do they fall?

- What is the overall dynamic curve shape of the whole show?

- What modes of enunciation are predominant in the score? Where in the dynamic curve do they sit for each moment, and how do they effect the intensification of each moment along the dynamic curve?

- What kind of highpoints are those in the show? Highpoints of lyricism? Spectacle? Intimacy?

- Are there any extroversive references in the score as a whole? Are there any associations that already exist in the world that are being played upon at any moment in the show and score?

The column method

As we saw with the Lévi-Strauss method in Chapter 4, list out the key narrative moments of the story. They should go in chronological order horizontally, but be placed into vertical columns that are grouped according to themes as they seem to arise as you go through the narrative.

At the end of this exercise, survey the columns and see how the narrative groups into themes (there are usually about four or five). It is likely that these are your trunk themes. Discuss as a team – do they feel right as your primary themes?

Sticky notes moments part 1

Using coloured sticky notes, write individual 'moments' that happen in the story for the show and lay them on a large surface in any order.

Keep the moments that are happening in your show's plot and remove those that are not. Add in any additional plot moments that are happening, and re-order the sticky notes so that they reflect your plot. If you are responsible for, or collaborating on, the show's plot, then play with the ordering of the plot moments by moving the sticky notes around, to see what happens when you tell the story in different way. If you are composing for a script that has already been written, or that has a writer who is creating the shape of the plot in this way, then skip to the point at which the sticky notes are reflecting the plot broken down in the order of the show.

Once you have all your narrative beats represented by sticky notes, line them up in a straight line side-by-side in show order.

Sticky notes moments part 2

Take a different coloured sticky note and place one with each narrative beat sticky note that you think should have song as a part of its expression. Have a look at the visual representation of that with the whole show laid out on the surface. Do they look well spaced? What is the role of song in the show? Is it playing a vital part in the storytelling? Does it provide commentary? Make sure that the songs are in places which align with what your whole team think the role of song is in the show.

In order to make this decision, consider the following questions:

- What is the function of music in your show as a whole? This is a two-part question:

  - First, what kind of show are you creating? Do the songs function in the context of a book musical where songs will occur in the midst of scenes? Or is the approach to have more integrated extended musical sequences as an umbrella for dialogue and song? Or is it a song cycle? Or is it a through-composed narrative musical, in which case most of your dynamic curve would be marked as being in song?

  - Second, given the answer to the question above, what dramatic role does music have in the show? For example, is it to give commentary in a direct address way to what is going on? Does it allow characters to express their inner thoughts? Do the songs happen within the context of the characters' daily life, or stand outside of that?

- How do the answers to the questions above affect which parts of the plot should be told through song?

You can repeat this exercise for other performance elements (dance, puppetry, projections, etc.).

Discuss each moment with your collaborators and reach agreement of how all of the performance elements are working together.

The highpoints

Looking at your narrative laid out on the surface, take it in turns to identify which moments you think are the highpoints. If there is disagreement, discuss between you until there is a consensus about which are the highpoints of the show (there should only be very few of them).

Remember Agawu's three definitions of a highpoint from p. 113

- 'A point of extreme tension'

- 'the site of a decisive release of tension'

- 'A turning point in the form'

Which are yours?

When you have decided, move these sticky notes up on the surface so that they are sitting at a significantly higher placed level than the rest of the sticky notes.

Given the dramatic context and scenario, is each of your highpoints going to be characterized as a highpoint of:

- Intensity?

- Lyricism?

- Spectacle?

- Intimacy?

How will you work with each of the elements of music to reflect that?

How will the performance modes work together to achieve that?

The big dynamic curve

You currently have the show's units mapped out by sticky notes with some raised as the highpoints. Now, together, reposition the other sticky notes into an approximation of how the units might rise and fall in intensification to reach the highpoints.

Now take a large piece of plain, or graph, paper, sketch a dynamic curve of the shape of the show so far, transferring what you have represented by the positioning of sticky notes into a line drawing that rises and falls with the levels of intensification. The horizontal axis represents time and the vertical axis represents the rise and fall of intensification. Remember from Parts One and Two of this book that it is up to you to decide the parameters by which that intensification is defined.

Draw small lines along the horizontal axis to indicate where each of the narrative units are, and label them accordingly.

Now mark on the shape where you think there should be songs.

If you are working in a group, or collaboratively with a choreographer, you may also wish to mark on the dynamic curve where dance is happening as well. Similar questions may be asked concerning what the role of dance in the show is and how it contributes to storytelling.

Refer back to the intensification chart on p. 83.

- Are there any other levels of heightening of the form here that are relevant to your show?

- Is it helpful to mark in where there should be underscore?

- Or are there significant visual or technical moments that need to be marked in?

- Do any of these also occur with music at the same time?

- How do your performance modes combine such that there is a multilayering of heightened mode?

Given all of these markings on your dynamic curve, does it now change its shaping? What impact are the decisions about performance modes and the placing of their heightening having on the shape of the show? Are there moments that are now heightened beyond the level of the plot because of their performance modes?

You've identified your highpoint(s) and their characteristics. You've also got a rough shape sketch of the whole show. Go back to this now, and consider the inclines and declining slopes that aren't highpoints. Take each of your narrative moments and decide whether it is:

- Exposition material or development material

- Is it on the way up? On the way down? Or does it plateau for a while?

Use this as the opportunity to interrogate each of your narrative units and decide:

a   What function each of the narrative units has in this way

b   Therefore, how steep a ramp up or down the shape might be on your way to the next 'landing point'.

Finally, check over the dynamic curve shape of your whole show.

- Do a pass looking over the curve that checks for the emotional storytelling of the piece – does the curve of that work?

- Do a pass looking over the curve that checks for the action in the piece, and where this is most tense – does that work?

- Check that you are happy with the relative balance between intensity of action and intensity of emotion. Has one been prioritized over the other, and if so, is that the right call for your specific show?

Finally, as the composer, it can be helpful to extract from the show's overall dynamic curve one that represents the score alone so that you have in mind the shaping of your score and the intensity of songs relative to each other on that curve. Put markers along the bottom horizontal axis that label the musical moments and then try to draw a curve that charts musical moment to moment, so you can see the musical shape of the piece.

Modes of enunciation

Review the definitions of the three modes of enunciation from Chapter 6. Is there a dramaturgical reason why any of them should be more prevalent than others in your musical?

Make a list of all of your song or musical moments. Next to each, write whether the song's intention is:

1   To inform or tell

2   To affect

3   To drive

This should help you decide whether each of the songs is in speech, song or dance mode. Make a note by each song according to its mode of enunciation.

As you are doing this, be aware if any of your ideas are drawing on connotations of something from the outside world. If so mark it with an 'E', standing for 'extroversive semiosis' and a note of what it is drawing on and why.

If you are working collaboratively in a group, this whole exercise can be extended to all of the sections in your show: repeat the process for dialogue scenes and for dance moments.

Have a look down your column of modes of enunciation:

- Does this seem balanced?
- Does it seem to make sense in terms of the dramatic needs of your show?
- Is there a specific character or strand of plot line which would make sense to be told via a particular mode of enunciation?
- Is there a lot of one kind of mode of enunciation (if so, contrast will be needed in other ways)?

Where in your show might there be songs that need to have a mixed mode of enunciation? Why might that be? What is it that means that is helpful dramatically?

Review your dynamic curve from the previous set of exercises and adjust it according to where you think the modes of enunciation might have an impact on the heightened intensity of any one particular moment or region.

Now that you have your list, and your final dynamic curve for the show, have a think about the musical elements for each song. Given the overall style, feel and genre of your show, which elements are going to help you with the function of speech, song or dance mode for each of your songs?

Layer three: The OS map

The OS map is worked out on a song-by-song basis. You can apply these same questions and same exercises to each song across the musical.

Primary questions

- Taking each song moment in turn, which song structures are you going to use for each musical moment?

- How do songs relate to each other across a thematic or character strand?

- Taking each character, which Laban efforts are most useful to you to conceptualize their personality? How does this affect their music? Which elements of music is this most conveyed through?

- Taking each song, which Laban efforts are helpful according to the specific drama of the moment? What mood are you trying to convey, and how does each element of music help you to do so?

- How does your accompanimental pattern relate to the vocal line, and what is the drama that each is telling per song?

Song structures

This is an exercise to do with words writer and composer together. You might discuss it, or you might each do your own version and compare notes.

Choose one of your key song moments. Briefly scribble down the story of that song: what is being conveyed in the song? What is the thought process of the character singing it? What needs to happen in the song? What needs to be different by the end of the song compared with at the beginning? You can do this as a freestyle monologue as if in the voice of your character, or you could do it in the third person, objectively writing down what happens.

Take some different coloured sticky strips, or different coloured pens. Read back over the story of your song with these questions in mind:

- When is there a new thought which takes us into a new topic?

- Is there one that keeps coming back?

Each time it feels like there is a change of train of thought, either put a sticky strip down, or underline that moment. Use the colours to group different kinds of thoughts. When it is a new kind of thought on a topic that has not been visited yet in the song, start a new colour; when a topic is returned to, return to that colour.

If the colours represent the sections of the song, what song structure seems to be emerging?

- Is there a topic that keeps coming back which might feel like a chorus for example?

- Is there a strong sense of change of direction part of the way through that feels like it might be a bridge, or leaning towards an AABA structure?

- Is the character stuck on a loop and so a strophic (AAA) structure might feel appropriate?

- Or are there multiple new thoughts throughout and the song feels like it might need to be through-composed?

An exercise such as this will allow the appropriate song structure to grow out of the dramatic story needing to happen within the song.

Exploring Laban efforts in music

This exercise can be adapted according to whether or not there are performers in your group. It is also a good exercise to bring together bookwriter, lyricist and composer (whether this is a group of people, three people, two or just one person).

Choose a small piece of one character's dialogue from the show; try to make it one which encapsulates their personality and is not unusual for that character – it is them in their everyday state. Consider from the list of Laban efforts below (or by performing it using differing versions of time, space and weight) which Laban effort you think that character is portraying in that moment.

Now choose a lyric that that character sings and try the same thing: which effort are they portraying? Is that the same as their book character's effort? If not, is there a specific dramatic reason why in this moment they might be different? Again, try to select material that will help get to the baseline effort for that character.

Once you have established what you all think the character's fundamental effort is, try to complete a version of the chart below. Based on the characteristics of time, space and weight of that particular effort, see how you think that might 'translate' into music.

Character's effort in this song:
Time (quick or sustained):
Space (direct or indirect):
Weight (heavy or light):

Musical element	Possible characteristics
Melody	
Tempo	
Rhythm	
Tonality	
Harmony	
Texture	
Orchestration and timbre	
Accompanimental pattern	

Composers

Once you have figured out the potential musical parameters and boundaries, compose the theme that might most encapsulate that character.

You can repeat this exercise for each character as their fundamental state, and also use it as a reference for how parameters might need to be altered when the character is in certain other scenarios or dramatic situations.

Song network

Revisit your song list from the exercise in the base map. You may be familiar with the sight of a patch bay that connects leads from outputs to inputs in a recording studio. The idea of this exercise is to create a network of connecting lines between the songs that are related to each other.

Songs may be related to each other by theme or by character: mark up your list however it is most helpful to you, to have a visual reference to make connections between songs that are related to each other.

Composing exercise: Accompaniments

Accompaniments can contain as much musical storytelling as do the vocal lines.

Choose one of your melodic themes (or the one you composed for the earlier exercise). As an exercise, without changing the melody itself, create the accompaniments that might recontextualize this musical theme if the character were:

a Angry

b Bored and longing for something to change

c Continually distracted by something out of the corner of their eye

d Emotionally affected by the memory that what they are singing about conjures in their mind

Note which element(s) of the music you are changing for each scenario. Are there some where you are changing all of the elements except the pitches and rhythm of the melody itself?

Layer four: The street map

The street map looks at the smallest units in the musical, exploring phrase shapes, and motivic musical manipulation and variation. The nature of the street map means that most of these exercises are mostly for the composer(s), although discussion around the branch themes and how they are related to trunk themes may be beneficial to do collaboratively.

Primary questions

- In each song, how does the phrase shaping work? Dramatically should they be short? Long? Fairly flat or undulating in shape? Why so?

- What are the branch themes in the show and how do they relate to the trunk themes? Do they relate to specific trunk theme songs or is there a shared palette of material throughout the show?

- On a small-scale level, what is the relationship between the vertical aspects of your score and the horizontal? How do harmony and melody relate to each other? What story is being told by that decision?

- Where might it make sense dramaturgically for small musical motifs and cells to be related to others?

- What are your key musical motifs and cells for the show?

- How might they be varied, musically manipulated and played with in order to spin more musical material?

- What are the different techniques you can use to spin small-scale musical material?

Composing exercise: Composing to shapes

As an exercise, draw a small dynamic curve shape. You could even start with the classic, basic dynamic curve shape from p. 76.

Now, following the contours of that shape, compose a short melody that reflects it. This can be as short as one phrase length.

Try this out with various different quickly sketched shapes.

Now choose a small unit of narrative from your show and sketch the shape that best seems to represent the natural shape of the dynamic intensification of the moment. Repeat the exercise with this shape, composing a short unit of musical material to the shape. Does it imply a sense of call and response with two short phrases? Or does it imply a more meandering, seeking, longer phrase?

Now consider the Laban effort that is also appropriate for this moment or character. If you bring that into the mix as well as the shape, how does that alter things? Try composing a section while considering both factors.

Back to the network

This exercise involves collaboratively looking back over a couple of earlier exercises and bringing them together:

a Your list of trunk themes from the base map

b Your song network list that shows songs that may be related to each other in some way

Consider each of the narrative trunk themes from the base map. Discuss other, tangential themes that you think are relevant to your show that result from each of these trunk themes. In other words, what are your branch themes? You might like to mind map these, so that the branch themes radiate out on the page from each trunk theme in the centre.

Sometimes it can be the case that branch themes create an implied network through the score, whereby songs that are in some way tangentially related to the core trunk themes of the show create a strand. Review your song network list with this in mind, noting where there might be branch themes in play. See whether this alters which songs you think might be related tangentially to each other.

Composing exercise: Creating cells

This exercise implies a method whereby you have composed, or part-composed, the songs related to the main trunk themes of your show first. This may not necessarily be the case. Even if it is not, doing this kind of exercise can still help to generate a wider palette of musical material for your show which is all in some way tangentially related to each other and the same soundworld.

I would often have a song that most encapsulates the core of each trunk theme. If this is the case for you, are you able to identify which songs these are? Within these songs, what are the main musical hooks?

On manuscript, or in a sequencer – however you work best – create a list of these handful of key musical themes to your show.

Now try going through the exercise of creating a series of derivations of them in the following ways. Take one phrase or unit of music that makes sense for you and try the following:

a   Write it out or play it into the sequencer, in retrograde (i.e. backwards)

b   Now in inversion. This is where you start on the same note but you invert each interval – if the original melody first of all goes up a tone, your inverted step is down a tone and so on throughout the whole melody.

c   Now augment the original melody, so that each of the note values becomes at least twice the length.

d   A further step on from this: now make that augmented melody a bassline. Try building a chord progression on top of that new bassline – does any part of it give a coherent, satisfying sense of chord progression that might be a good way of embedding previously heard melodic material within a tangentially related song by making it the foundation of the harmony?

e   Another version of this kind of idea: take three or more notes that are next to each other in sequence in the theme's melody, and play them all at once so that they become a chord. Are there any progressions contained within your original theme's melody where melody could become harmony (often scrunchy harmony) in this way that sounds satisfying? It might be there is just one small section of your melody that this might work for.

f   Now try your thematic melody in diminution; that is where the note values are at least halved. Try creating a cell like this of material in diminution that could repeat as a riff. Could this now become an accompanimental pattern for another song?

We're now going to fragment the trunk themes: see where you can split them up into small cells, characteristic interval jumps or little motifs. Now, make a list of these so that you have a whole palette of small motifs.

You can now apply the above steps a–f with any of your small, fragmented cells as well. In addition to this, try taking one of the small fragments and then allowing the melody to veer off in a different direction to the original: it might begin with the same cell but then go somewhere else musically after that.

We can see that by these means, as well as by making changes to individual elements of the same musical material as we did in exercise 4 of the OS map, we can arrive in a position of having a wide palette of musical material to play with. This exercise, in a sense, is endless. You can try it with every trunk theme in the show. You can then spin more material from the derived material from a first spinning. All of this can be used as a palette of shared material, like the musical bank for the whole show and the characters within it who share the same inhabited world. Or you can use it in a strategic way, whereby different derivations of a particular trunk theme can be used for songs that are tangentially related, bringing about a sense of subtle cohesion to a strand of musical storytelling, without an overt sense of reprise (much as you may wish to use reprise when the dramatic moment calls for it). It is also a reminder that you don't need to be coming up with absolutely new material for every single song. Once the trunk building blocks of your score are in place, so much can come from carefully working with this material; breaking it down and remoulding its components so that each moment sounds fresh and yet somehow cohesive in relationships between the songs.

With all of the building blocks in place, you have everything you need to create the score and be the composer as dramatist.

***

I hope your passion for musical theatre continues to grow, as we all find ever-evolving and exciting new ways to tell stories through the relationship between music and drama.

References

35MM: A Musical Exhibition 2012. [Original Cast Recording].

Agawu, K., 1984. Structural Highpoints in Schumann's *Dichterliebe*. *Music Analysis*, 3(2), pp. 159–80.

Agawu, K., 1992. Theory and Practice in the Analysis of the Nineteenth-Century Lied. *Music Analysis*, 11(1), pp. 3–36.

Agawu, K., 2009. *Music as Discourse: Semiotic Adventures in Romantic Music*. Oxford: Oxford University Press.

Barthes, R., 1977. *Image, Music, Text*. London: Fontana Press.

Barthes, R., 2000. *Mythologies*. London: Vintage Books.

Billy Elliot: The Musical Live 2014. [Film] Dir. Stephen Daldry, UK: Universal Pictures.

Bonnie, L., 2014. 'Jason Robert Brown Exclusive Interview – The Last Five Years', 8 September. Available online: https://www.youtube.com/watch?v=eo_3feEG4D0 (accessed 16 February 2022).

CBS, 2008. 'Elton on "Billy Elliot"', 30 October. Available online: https://www.youtube.com/watch?v=REa2EWd9Bzg (accessed 15 February 2022).

Chatman, S., 1980. *Story and Discourse: Narrative Structure in Fiction and Film*. Ithaca: Cornell University Press.

Cohan, S. and Shires, L., 1988. *Telling Stories: A Theoretical Analysis of Narrative Fiction*. Abingdon: Routledge.

Come From Away 2017. [Original Broadway Cast Recording].

Dear Evan Hansen 2021. [Film] Dir. Stephen Chbosky, Universal Pictures.

Engel, L., 2006. *Words with Music: Creating the Broadway Musical Libretto*. Minnesota: Hal Leonard Corporation.

Everybody's Talking About Jamie 2018. [Original West End Cast Recording].

Everybody's Talking About Jamie 2021. [Film] Dir. Jonathan Butterell. California: Amazon Studios.

Fun Home 2014. [Original Cast Recording].

Guettel, A. & Lucas, C., 2014. *The Light in the Piazza*. New York: Theatre Communications Group.

Hadestown 2019. [Original Broadway Cast Recording].

In the Heights 2008. [Original Broadway Cast Recording].

In the Heights 2021. [Film] Dir. Jon M. Chu. United States: Warner Bros. Pictures.

Jamie.musical, 2001. 'Matt and Grace Interview Dan Gillespie-Sells (Everybody's Talking About Jamie)'. Available online: https://www.youtube.com/watch?v=_tNf3GZwhwM (accessed 13 March 2022).

Knowles, R., 2014. *How Theatre Means*. Basingstoke: Palgrave Macmillan.

Kron, L. & Tesori, J., 2017. *Fun Home Vocal Selections*. New York: Samuel French.

The Last Five Years 2014. [Film] Dir. Richard LaGravenese, Radius-TWC.

The Last Ship 2014. [Original Broadway Cast Recording].

Lévi-Strauss, C., 1955. The Structural Study of Myth. *The Journal of American Folklore,* 68(270), Myth: A Symposium (Oct–Dec, 1955), pp. 428–44.

Lévi-Strauss, C., 1983. *The Raw and the Cooked*. Chicago: University of Chicago Press.

The Light in the Piazza 2005. [Original Broadway Cast Recording].

London Road 2015. [Film] UK: Picturehouse Entertainment.

MacRae, T. & Gillespie Sells D., 2017. *Everybody's Talking About Jamie: Vocal Selections*. London: Samuel French Inc.

Marlow, T. & Moss, L., 2020. *Six: The Musical Songbook*. London: Faber Music Ltd.

Matilda the Musical 2013. [Original Broadway Cast Recording].

McMillin, S., 2006. *The Musical as Drama*. Princeton: Princeton University Press.

Melrose, S., 1994. *A Semiotics of the Dramatic Text*. Basingstoke: The Macmillan Press.

Minchin, T., 2012. *Matilda the Musical Piano Vocal Selections*. Toronto: Wise Publications.

Miranda, L-M., 2008. *In the Heights: Vocal Selections*. Nashville: Williamson Music.

Mitchell, A., 2021. *Hadestown: Vocal Selections*. Milwaukee: Hal Leonard.

Mordden, E., 2015. *On Sondheim: An Opinionated Guide*. Oxford: Oxford University Press.

Official London Theatre, 2019. 'Interview with the Writers of *Six the Musical* Toby Marlow and Lucy Moss', 14 January. Available online: https://www.youtube.com/watch?v=YNIFnQVRoRg (accessed 30 January 2022).

Oliver, R. S., 2012. *35MM: A Musical Exhibition Vocal Selections*. New York: Samuel French Inc.

Playhouse Square, 2016. 'Fun Home: An Interview with Jeanine Tesori'. 27 September. Available online: https://www.youtube.com/watch?v=W4A7wrXoJ64 (accessed 15 February 2022).

Siropoulos, V., 2010. Evita, the Society of the Spectacle and the Advent of the Megamusical. *Image and Narrative*, 11(2), pp. 165–76.

Six 2019. [Original Cast Recording] Absolute.

Sue Townsend's *The Secret Diary of Adrian Mole Aged 133/4 The Musical* 2019. [Original London Cast Recording].

Swain, J., 2002. *The Broadway Musical: A Critical and Musical Survey*. Maryland: The Scarecrow Press.

Talks at Google, 2009. 'Broadway's Hadestown', 8 May. Available online: https://www.youtube.com/watch?v=foMPZggeAN0&t=1594s (accessed 14 February 2022).

Whisper House 2009. [Album].

Woolford, J., 2012. *How Musicals Work: And How to Write Your Own*. London: Nick Hern Books.

Bibliography

35MM: A Musical Exhibition 2012. [Original Cast Recording].

Abbate, C., 1996. *Unsung Voices: Opera and Musical Narrative in the Nineteenth Century.* Princeton: Princeton University Press.

Almén, B., 2003. Narrative Archetypes: A Critique, Theory and Method of Narrative Analysis. *Journal of Music Theory*, 47(1), pp. 1–39.

Agawu, K., 1984. Structural Highpoints in Schumann's *Dichterliebe. Music Analysis*, 3(2), pp. 159–80.

Agawu, K., 1992. Theory and Practice in the Analysis of the Nineteenth-Century Lied. *Music Analysis*, 11(1), pp. 3–36.

Agawu, K., 1997. Analysing Music under the New Musicological Regime. *The Journal of Musicology*, 15(3), pp. 297–307.

Agawu, K., 2009. *Music as Discourse: Semiotic Adventures in Romantic Music.* Oxford: Oxford University Press.

Agawu, K., 2014. *Playing with Signs: A Semiotic Interpretation of Classical Music.* Princeton: Princeton University Press.

Altman, R. ed., 1981. *Genre: The Musical.* Boston: Routledge and Kegan Paul.

Andrews, R., 1997. *Writing a Musical.* London: Robert Hale.

Aston, E. and Savona, G., 1991. *Theatre as Sign-System: A Semiotics of Text and Performance.* London: Routledge.

Bal, M., 1997. *Narratology: Introduction to the Theory of Narrative.* Toronto: University of Toronto Press.

Barthes, R., 1977. *Image, Music, Text.* London: Fontana Press.

Barthes, R., 2000. *Mythologies.* London: Vintage Books.

Barthes, R., and Duisit, L., 1975. An Introduction to the Structural Study of Narrative. *New Literary History*, 6(2), pp. 237–72.

Billy Elliot: The Musical Live 2014. [Film] Dir. Stephen Daldry, UK: Universal Pictures.

Bonnie, L., 2014. 'Jason Robert Brown Exclusive Interview – The Last Five Years', 8 September. Available online: https://www.youtube.com/watch?v=eo_3feEG4D0 (accessed 16 February 2022).

Bordwell, D., 2009. *Making Meaning.* Harvard: Harvard University Press.

Bruce, M., 2016. *Writing Music for the Stage: A Practical Guide for Theatremakers.* London: Nick Hern.

Campbell, J., 2008. *The Hero with a Thousand Faces.* Novato: New World Library.

Carlson, M., 1990. *Theatre Semiotics: Signs of Life.* Bloomington and Indianapolis: Indiana University Press.

CBS, 2008. 'Elton on "Billy Elliot"', 30 October. Available at https://www.youtube.com/watch?v=REa2EWd9Bzg (accessed 15 February).

Chambers, R., 1984. *Story and Situation: Narrative Seduction and the Power of Fiction.* Minneapolis: University of Minnesota Press.

Chatman, S., 1980. *Story and Discourse: Narrative Structure in Fiction and Film.* Ithaca: Cornell University Press.

Chatman, S., 1981. Reply to Barbara Herrnstein Smith. *Critical Inquiry,* 7(4), p. 802.

Chatman, S., 1990. *Coming to Terms: The Rhetoric of Narrative in Fiction.* Ithaca: Cornell University Press.

Cohan, S. and Shires, L., 1988. *Telling Stories: A Theoretical Analysis of Narrative Fiction.* Abingdon: Routledge.

Cohan, S. ed., 2010. *The Sound of Musicals.* London: Palgrave Macmillan.

Cohen, A. J., 2001. Music as a Source of Emotion in Film. In Juslin, P. and Sloboda, J. eds., *Music and Emotion: Theory and Research.* Oxford: Oxford University Press. pp. 249–72.

Cohen, A. & Rosenhaus, S., 2016. *Writing Musical Theater.* New York: Palgrave Macmillan.

Come From Away 2017. [Original Broadway Cast Recording].

Cook, N., 2000. *Analysing Musical Multimedia.* Oxford: Oxford University Press.

Cook, N., 2001. Theorizing Musical Meaning. *Music Theory Spectrum,* 23(2), pp. 170–95.

Dahlhaus, C., 1989. What Is a Musical Drama? *Cambridge Opera Journal,* 1, p. 95.

Dear Evan Hansen 2021. [film] Dir. Stephen Chbosky. United States: Universal Pictures.

Dundes, A., 1997. Binary Opposition in Myth: The Propp/Lévi-Strauss Debate in Retrospect. *Western Folklore,* 56(1), pp. 39–50.

Dyer, R., 2002. *Only Entertainment.* Abingdon: Routledge.

Eco, U., 1976. *A Theory of Semiotics.* Bloomington: Indiana University Press.

Engel, L., 2006. *Words with Music: Creating the Broadway Musical Libretto.* Minnesota: Hal Leonard Corporation.

Everybody's Talking About Jamie. 2018. [Original West End Cast Recording].

Everybody's Talking About Jamie. 2021 [Film] Dir. Jonathan Butterell. California: Amazon Studios.

Feuer, J., 1977. The Self-Reflective Musical and the Myth of Entertainment. *Quarterly Review of Film Studies,* 2(3), pp. 313–26.

Feuer, J., 1982. *The Hollywood Musical.* Bloomington: Indiana University Press.

Fortier, M., 1997. *Theory/Theatre an Introduction.* London: Routledge.

Frankel, A., 2009. *Writing the Broadway Musical.* Boston: Da Capo Press.

Fun Home. 2014. [Original Cast Recording].

Genette, G., 1980. *Narrative Discourse.* Oxford: Basil Blackwell.

Gottdiener, M., 1985. Hegemony and Mass Culture: A Semiotic Approach. *The American Journal of Sociology,* 90(5), pp. 979–1001.

Gottfried, M., 1984. *Broadway Musicals.* New York: Abradale Press.

Greimas, A. J., 1987. *On Meaning: Selected Writings in Semiotic Theory.* Minneapolis: University of Minnesota Press.

Greimas, A. J., 1989. Narrative Grammar: Units and Levels. *MLN,* 86(6), pp. 793–806.

Guettel, A. & Lucas, C., 2014. *The Light in the Piazza*. New York: Theatre Communications Group.

Hadestown [Original Cast Recording].

Hatten, R., 2004. *Interpreting Musical Gestures, Topics and Tropes: Mozart, Beethoven, Schubert*. Bloomington: Indiana University Press.

Hernstein Smith, B., 1980. Narrative Versions, Narrative Theories. *Critical Inquiry*, 7(1), pp. 213–36.

Hirsch, F., 1989. *Harold Prince and the American Musical Theatre*. Cambridge: Cambridge University Press.

In the Heights 2008. [Original Broadway Cast Recording].

In the Heights 2021. [Film] Dir. Jon M. Chu. United States: Warner Bros. Pictures.

Jamie.musical, 2001. 'Matt and Grace Interview Dan Gillespie-Sells (Everybody's Talking About Jamie)'. Available online: https://www.youtube.com/watch?v=_tNf3GZwhwM (accessed 13 March 2022).

Kirle, B., 2005. *Unfinished Show Business*. Carbondale: Southern Illinois Press.

Kislan, R., 1980. *The Musical: A Look at the American Musical Theatre*. New Jersey: Prentice-Hall.

Kivy, P., 1984. *Sound and Semblance: Reflections on Musical Representation*. Princeton: Princeton University Press.

Knapp, R., 2005. *The American Musical Theatre and the Formation of National Identity*. Princeton: Princeton University Press.

Knapp, R., 2006. *The American Musical and the Performance of Personal Identity*. Princeton: Princeton University Press.

Knowles, R., 2014. *How Theatre Means*. Basingstoke: Palgrave Macmillan.

Kron, L. & Tesori, J., 2017. *Fun Home Vocal Selections*. New York: Samuel French.

Lamb, A., 2000. *150 Years of Popular Musical Theatre*. Yale: Yale University Press.

The Last Five Years 2014. [film] Dir. Richard LaGravenese Radius-TWC.

The Last Ship 2014. [Original Broadway Cast Recording].

Lawson-Peebles, R., 1996. *Approaches to the American Musical*. Exeter: University of Exeter Press.

Lerner, A., 1989. *The Musical Theatre: A Celebration*. Boston: Da Capo Press.

Lévi-Strauss, C., 1983. *The Raw and the Cooked*. Chicago: University of Chicago Press.

Lévi-Strauss, C., 1955. The Structural Study of Myth. *The Journal of American Folklore*, 68(270), Myth: A Symposium (Oct–Dec, 1955), pp. 428–44.

The Light in the Piazza 2005. [Original Broadway Cast Recording].

London Road 2015. [film] UK: Picturehouse Entertainment.

Lothe, J., 2000. *Narrative in Fiction and Film*. Oxford: Oxford University Press.

MacRae, T. & Gillespie Sells D., 2017. *Everybody's Talking About Jamie: Vocal Selections*. London: Samuel French Inc.

Matilda the Musical 2013. [Original Broadway Cast Recording].

Marlow, T. & Moss, L., 2020. *Six: The Musical Songbook*. London: Faber Music Ltd.

Mast, G., 1987. *Can't Help Singin': The American Musical on Stage and Screen*. New York: Overlook Press.

Melrose, S., 1994. *A Semiotics of the Dramatic Text*. Basingstoke: The Macmillan Press.

McMillin, S., 2006. *The Musical as Drama*. Princeton: Princeton University Press.

McPherson, B., 2014. Dynamic Shape: The Dramaturgy of Song and Dance in Lloyd Webber's *Cats*. In Symonds, D. and Taylor, M. eds., *Gestures of Music Theatre*. New York: Oxford University Press. Ch. 4. pp. 54–69.

McQuillan, M., 2000. *The Narrative Reader*. London: Routledge.

Minchin, T., 2012. *Roald Dahl's Matilda: The Musical Vocal Selections*. Toronto: Wise Publications.

Miranda, L-M., 2008. *In the Heights: Vocal Selections*. Nashville: Williamson Music.

Mitchell, A., 2021. *Hadestown: Vocal Selections*. Milwaukee: Hal Leonard.

Mitchell, W. J. T., 1981. *On Narrative*. Chicago: University of Chicago Press.

Mordden, E., 1981. *The American Theatre*. Oxford: Oxford University Press.

Mordden, E., 2015. *On Sondheim: An Opinionated Guide*. Oxford: Oxford University Press.

Mosley, D., 1990. *Gesture, Sign and Song*. New York: Peter Lang Publishing.

Nattiez, J-J., 1990. Can One Speak of Narrativity in Music? *Journal of the Royal Musical Association*, 115(2), pp. 240–57.

Neale, S., 1990. Questions of Genre. In Stam, R. and Miller, T. eds., 2000. *Film and Theory an Anthropology*. Oxford: Blackwell Publishers. Ch.10.

Newlove, J., 2007. *Laban for Actors and Dancers: Putting Laban's Movement Theory into Practice: A Step-by-step Guide*. London: Nick Hern.

Newlove, J. & Dalby, J., 2019. *Laban for All*. New York: Taylor & Francis.

Noske, F., 1990. *The Signifier and the Signified: Studies in the Operas of Mozart and Verdi*. Oxford: Clarendon Press.

Official London Theatre, 2019. 'Interview with the Writers of *Six the Musical* Toby Marlow and Lucy Moss', 14 January. Available online: https://www.youtube.com/watch?v=YNIFnQVRoRg (accessed 30 January 2022).

Oliver, R. S., 2012. *35MM: A Musical Exhibition Vocal Selections*. New York: Samuel French Inc.

Pavis, P., 1981. Problems of a Semiology of Theatrical Gesture. *Poetics Today*, 2(3), pp. 65–93.

Pavis, P., 2001. Theatre Studies and Interdisciplinarity. *Theatre Research International*, 26(2), pp. 153–63.

Playhouse Square, 2016. 'Fun Home: An Interview with Jeanine Tesori', 27 September. Available online: https://www.youtube.com/watch?v=W4A7wrXoJ64 (accessed 15 February 2022).

Quinn, M. L., 1995. *The Semiotic Stage*. New York: Peter Lang Publishing.

Rodgers, R., 2002. *Musical Stages*. Cambridge: Da Capo Press.

Savran, D., 2004. Toward a Historiography of the Popular. *Theatre Survey*, 45(2), pp. 211–17.

Schleifer, R., 1987. *A.J. Greimas and the Nature of Meaning*. London: Croom Helm.

Scholes, R., & Kellogg, R., 1966. *The Nature of Narrative*. Oxford: Oxford University Press.

Shepherd, J., 1994. Music, Culture and Interdisciplinarity: Reflections on Relationships. *Popular Music*, 13(2), pp. 127–41.

Siropoulos, V., 2010. Evita, the Society of the Spectacle and the Advent of the Megamusical. *Image and Narrative*, 11(2), pp. 165–76.

Siropoulos, V., 2010. Cats, Postdramatic Blockbuster Aesthetics and the Triumph of the Megamusical. *Image and Narrative*, 11(3), pp. 128–45.

Siropoulos, V., 2011. Megamusicals, Spectacle and the Postdramatic Aesthetics of Late Capitalism. *Studies in Musical Theatre*, 5(1), pp. 13–34.

Six 2019. [Original Cast Recording] Absolute.

Spencer, D., 2005. *The Musical Theatre Writer's Survival Guide*. Portsmouth: Heinemann.

Stanzel, F. K., 1984. *A Theory of Narrative*. Cambridge: Cambridge University Press.

Stempel, L., 1992. The Musical Play Expands. *American Music*, 10(2), pp. 136–69.

Sternfeld, J., 2006. *The Megamusical*. Minneapolis: Indiana University Press.

Steyn, M., 2014. *Broadway Babies Say Goodnight*. London: Routledge.

Storey, J., 2006. *Cultural Theory and Popular Culture an Introduction*. Athens: University of Georgia Press.

Sue Townsend's *The Secret Diary of Adrian Mole Aged 13³ᐟ⁴ The Musical* 2019. [Original London Cast Recording].

Sutton, M., 1981. Patterns of Meaning in the Musical. In Altman, R. ed., 1981. *Genre: The Musical*. London: Routledge & Kegan Paul. pp. 190–6.

Swain, J., 2002. *The Broadway Musical: A Critical and Musical Survey*. Maryland: The Scarecrow Press.

Symonds, D. & Karantonis, P. eds., 2013. *The Legacy of Opera: Reading Music Theatre as Experience and Performance*. Amsterdam: Rodopi.

Symonds, D., 2005. Leap of Faith. PhD. Royal Holloway, University of London.

Symonds, D. & Taylor, M. eds., 2014. *Gestures of Music Theatre*. New York: Oxford University Press.

Tagg, P., 1987. Musicology and the Semiotics of Popular Music. *Semiotica*, 66(1/3), pp. 279–98.

Talks at Google, 2019. 'Broadway's Hadestown', 8 May. Available online: https://www.youtube.com/watch?v=foMPZggeAN0&t=1594s (accessed 14 February 2022).

Tarasti, E., 2002. *Signs of Music: A Guide to Musical Semiotics*. Boston: Walter de Gruyter.

de Toro, F., 1995. *Theatre Semiotics: Text and Staging in Modern Theatre*. Toronto: University of Toronto Press.

Whisper House 2009. [Album].

Winkler, E., 1990. *The Function of Song in Contemporary British Drama*. Newark: University of Delaware Press.

Woolford, J., 2012. *How Musicals Work: And How to Write Your Own*. London: Nick Hern Books.

Index

9 781350 229402